Mr. Irresponsible's Bad Advice

How to Rip the Lid Off Your Id and Live Happily Ever After

Mr. Irresponsible

as typed by

Bi

T0168101

Volt Press
Los Angeles

09 08 07 06 05   5 4 3 2 1

Library of Congress Cataloging-in-Publication Data

Barol, Bill, 1957-
  Mr. Irresponsible's bad advice : how to rip the lid off your Id and
  live happily ever after / by Mr. Irresponsible as typed by Bill
  Barol.
     p. cm.
  ISBN 1-56625-255-5
  1. Conduct of life—Humor. 2. Advice columns—Humor. I. Title.
  PN6231.C6142B37 2005
  814'.6--dc22
                              2005014831

Volt Press
A Division of Bonus Books, Inc.
9255 Sunset Blvd., #717
Los Angeles, CA 90069

Cover Photo: Gaku Shiroma
Cover and Book Design: Joy Jacob

Printed in the United States of America

For Jennifer

Table of Contents

About the Author

Mr. Irresponsible is the pen name of the world's most widely read personal advice columnist. His newspaper column, "Mr. Irresponsible's Bad Advice," ran in over 1,100 newspapers until early 2004, when it was suddenly and without explanation suspended by its syndicate. He is the recipient of the Heidelberg Prize, the Baxter Award (1987 and 1999) and the Lifetime Achievement Award of the Personal Improvement Institute, which he refused, sending a life-sized cutout of teen idol Justin Timberlake to the awards luncheon in his place.

Mr. Irresponsible has many enemies and must travel in disguise. He lives alone and likes it. Rumors that he "shot a man in Reno just to watch him die" have never been proven to have any basis in fact.

As of press time, Mr. Irresponsible is party to 19 different law suits, and is fighting to regain his newspaper column.

Introduction

It's long been my practice to avoid direct contact with the public, much as a conscientious lab worker might avoid actually touching the deadly bacteria that provide him his livelihood. Occasionally, though, a reader will pierce the veil of secrecy in which I live and approach me for advice. "Mr. Irresponsible," he'll ask, "how can I help my family navigate its way through the tricky thicket of today's ambiguous moral climate?" And I always explain to him: "'Tricky thicket'? Jesus, what are you, a Jumble puzzle? Talk normally, that's the first thing you should do. 'Tricky thicket.' *Jesus*." This gets his attention! Next I counsel him to "Get off my foot, take one step back and quit breathing through your mouth. You sound like Darth Vader." This is the part of the advice-giving process I like to think of as "Bringing The Pain©." It is generally greeted by a confused look, a twitch over the left or right brow, and an aimless flapping of the fingertips. "Look," I'll say next, "I don't mean to be rude," and I'll see his expression soften and a hopeful look come into his dim, narrow eyes. "But it looks like you do," I'll continue, adding: "Can't you see I'm working here?" (If on a personal errand, I may substitute appropriately: "Can't you see I'm picking out a bird-bath here?" Or: "Can't you see I'm having my car detailed?") Golly, the number of people who have actually started to physically back away from me at this point! "That's right," I always conclude encouragingly, "ask your little question and run away. Loser."

The point is, there is never a good time to ask advice. Particularly if you're asking it of me, with my busy schedule and many, many commitments. That's why I've taken the time to assemble this book of common-sense answers to many of modern life's most thorny dilemmas. Now, I know what you're thinking, because I always know what you're thinking, and don't look so impressed because frankly it isn't that tough. You're thinking, "Gosh, this Mr. Irresponsible fella seems a little . . . rough around the edges, I guess. A little . . . unkind." Which is precisely my point. You should be thinking, "Well, screw you, Jack." That's what I'd be thinking if some pseudonymous word-clown I didn't even know started popping off about how I should live my life. But instead you're thinking, "He strikes me as a little . . . I don't know, *abrupt* or something." You're actually thinking the ellipses, aren't you? You know why that is? Because you don't have the self-confidence to think a thought straight through to its logical conclusion. You have to stick that mewling little postmodern pause in there, that hitch in your thoughts that says, "I'm reflective, I'm . . . *thoughtful*." Well, you know what? "Reflective" and "thoughtful" mean the same thing, jackass. You can't even talk to yourself clearly, so how do you expect to talk to anybody else?

That little hitch is the great curse of our times. It's the pause that obscures, that separates us from our true natures. For what are we, really, if not the grumpy, snappish, easily annoyed kings and queens of the food chain? Consider the paramecium, as docile and socially cooperative a creature as has ever existed. It lives in the brackish water at the bottom of trout ponds. Now consider Mr. Irresponsible, a man who has spent the last two decades doling out spite in great huge bowlfuls. Do you know where Mr. Irresponsible lives? He lives in a split-level designer home on the 14th green of a PGA Tour golf course. I think you see my point: Crankiness is good. It is right. It is evolutionarily successful. If Mr. Irresponsible has a purpose in this world it's to reconnect you with what he likes to call the Inner Crank®, to remove that hitch from your thoughts, to liberate the straight-talking, consequences-be-damned Darwinian success story that lives in each of us. If Mr. Irresponsible has two purposes in this world, the second is to remain rich and famous enough that he can continue to refer to himself in the third person.

Which brings me to a personal note. After the very public unpleasantness which attended my firing from the newspaper column that had been my forum for over 25 years, I withdrew into a private period of introspection. This period lasted for 11 hours, including a four-hour nap and the 90 minutes it took to drive to Baskin-Robbins and back. At this point, energized and well-rested, I resolved to return to public life, and also to engage my former employers in a period of litigation so punishing and nightmarish that they would long for the sweet relief of death.

Predictably, they reacted like poor sports. My team of legal advisers advises me to refrain from comment on the specifics of the charges and countercharges which have since flown between our two camps. I plan to do so, except to say this: The materials found in my car were neither hallucinogens nor "massive quantities of Army-grade neurotoxins," as has been reported. The girl was over 18, and by precisely how much is irrelevant. She was at the time my research associate, and I have notarized documents to prove it. (She is also a notary.) The crate of automatic weapons in my trunk was sold to me on eBay as a "holiday grab bag" containing off-brand Slinkies and Mike Piazza bobble-head dolls. How the ferrets got into my house, I have no idea, nor do I know under what circumstances they were infected with Ebola. The notion that I would use the infected ferrets, automatic weapons, and "neurotoxins" to launch a convoluted scheme of revenge against my former publishers, with the girl as a stooge or henchman, is ludicrous, as is the assertion that the girl had been hypnotized by me, or by professional magicians hired by me, into uncritically doing my bidding. All these charges will be addressed in open court by my representatives.

In the meantime, I have decided to collect the best of my newspaper work in this book, annotating and expanding upon my original answers with wholly new advice. I feel that this is the best way to continue my life's work, as well as to circumvent copyright restrictions on the original material.

It's been said that "there is no problem so complex it can't be oversimplified," and I believe this maxim so deeply that in the absence of any hard evidence to the contrary I am prepared to claim authorship. This book represents the culmination of a lifetime's journey, an odyssey of thought, writing, and teaching on interpersonal relationships. I have been on that journey many, many years, and I intend to remain on it until the possibilities for spinoffs exhaust themselves. I hope you'll come along with me. Or don't. Either way, it's all the same to me.

Author's Note:

Introducing My Typist

When the judge in one of my suits against my former syndicate[1] ruled that neither I nor "any person hired by [me]" be allowed to touch a keyboard for the duration of the proceedings, the answer seemed simple: a helper monkey. With a few basic hand signals and a lot of bananas, I figured, I could end up with a more or less sentient typist who would be adequate for the relatively simple task of transcribing this book. Debbie's inquiries, however, proved futile. Apparently the tiny cabal of colorless bureaucrats who control access to trained assistance monkeys have their own small-minded "rules" for who may get one, and Rule #1 is that the creatures go exclusively to "people with problems."[2] A few follow-up calls found the same restriction placed on helper dogs, helper cats, helper voles,

....

1. Or it may have been one of the judges in one of the countersuits. Honestly, at this point I'm having trouble keeping track. I'm thinking about having my assistant Debbie make up some sort of color-coded chart.
2. Debbie emitted a brief, unpleasant snicker when she heard this and was promptly fired, but, as she explained at the time, "You've fired me so many times I don't even hear you anymore."

helper burros, helper parrots, helper bears, and helper sheep, as well as a small variety of "helper plants" being developed experimentally by a group at UC Santa Cruz.

With a deadline approaching and no monkey to be had, I was forced to go to my second choice: an unemployed screenwriter. That's how I came to be acquainted with Bill Barol, to whom I am dictating these words. The good news is, the system works more or less the same—we communicate largely by grunts and outsized gestures. Even better, as a screenwriter he seems afraid to bring up the subject of money. So far he seems content to work for sandwiches, which places us technically in compliance with the court order. Debbie, meanwhile, continues to try to line up a monkey.

Chapter

Manners

Teaching by "Hey!"

Imagine a world without manners. Surely this won't take you very long, because there is such a world, and it is called "Earth."

It wasn't always this way. Not so long ago men tipped their hats to ladies in the street, ladies curtsied in reply, and children were required by law to be courteous and respectful or risk a late-night incursion into their bedrooms by heavily armed Federal Manners Police bearing truncheons and the authority to use them against any young people who sulked, slouched, rolled their eyes, scuffed their giant chunky shoes against the pavement, or answered any adult question with the phrase "I dunno." These were glorious days! Sadly, those days are past.[3]

There's reason for hope, however. It's a slim hope, but is hope not, in the memorable formulation of the

....
3. Except in Malaysia.

Sorbonne's Dr. Emil Poutasse, the thing that pushes reason aside?[4] So I have reason to believe that we may once again become a well-mannered species. The key is the inculcation of manners into our kids, for they are both the hope of the species and the principal carriers of what might be called the "rudeness gene." Obviously, this will take some doing. But Mr. Irresponsible is here to help, via a simple pedagogical method I call Teaching by "Hey!" Let me explain.

I believe in the existence of what I call the "*Hey!*" Center®, which is that part of the primitive forebrain that in effect sits up and says "*Hey!*" in involuntary response to the application of a small amount of physical force. I have in my own research quantified this amount as one fF, or the amount of energy delivered by one finger-flick to the temple. This is a degree of force far too small to be painful or inflict injury, but just large enough to penetrate the fog of sensory overload in which we all live. Try this simple experiment now in your own home:

1. Sneak up behind an unsuspecting family member.

2. Reach around and flick this person smartly in the temple with your index or middle finger.

....

4. It seems a good thing, on reflection, that the rest of this quote is less well remembered: "L'espoir est la chose qui pousse la raison de côté, pousse l'amour et la haine au plancher, ne les aime pas partager avec envie et n'entre pas dans les allumettes de cri inutiles avec l'avarice." ("Hope is the thing that pushes reason aside, shoves love and hate to the floor, doesn't like to share with envy and gets into unnecessary shouting matches with greed.") Poutasse, it now seems clear, was quite insane.

My research indicates with 97 percent certainty that your family member will turn, an irritated look on his or her face, and say "*Hey!*" At that moment, you will have this person's full attention. You have reached what academics call "a teachable moment." (Catholic school teachers were historically among the first to recognize the efficacy of this method in a classroom setting.)

I believe that the "*Hey!*" Center® is, evolutionarily speaking, the locus of the annoyance response, and that the annoyance response is key to the advancement of our species. It is the physical seat of the impulses to "get steamed," to "swelter," to "smart off" and "crack wise," to "split the fish" and "roll the melon up the stairs." All of these impulses are healthy, as I've noted. Let's look at them in practice.

Let's Go Out to the Lobby and Get Ourselves Some Whoopass

In the fall of 1999 I received a letter from Mrs. A. O. of Elmira, N.Y., who asked:

> I am at my wit's end trying to
> teach my children, who are eight
> and six, some manners. My hus-
> band and I believe in teaching
> by example. So we try at every

opportunity to show our kids
how to be well-mannered. My
husband always holds the car
door open for me, I say "Bless
you" when someone sneezes in
a bank line, and so forth.
Unfortunately, none of this ever
seems to sink in with our kids.
Can you help?

Let me now expand on the answer I gave Mrs. A. O. in my column.

Holy cow, will you please shut up and quit whining? *Oh, my kids are such hellions. They're so rude and inconsiderate I just don't know what to do.* Well, you know what? I do. I had a good fix on your kids from the first sentence of your letter. By the second sentence I was ready to scream. By the third I was ready to hang myself. By the fourth I'd lost interest. It's a miracle the fifth sentence even registered on my retinas, because by the time you got to "Can you help?" the neural pathways had snapped shut and I was gone, baby, gone. It was only the sound of Debbie rapping on the edge of my desk that brought me back to reality, and that was just because it was time for lunch. Let me be clear about this, and I want to put it as kindly as possible: the pathetic tone of your sad little letter made me want to pummel you with a bat until I could hear the sound of bat on sidewalk.

It's no mystery how to teach little Jason and Tiffany some manners. (The only mystery is how they ever got to be eight and six with parents like you.) Here it is: Whatever you do, *don't teach by example*. Teaching by example is only a good idea if you're a homesteader family on the plains of Nebraska in 1888 and your kids have nothing else to do all day but sit back and study the way you and Paw interact with the world in the few idle moments when you're not busy trying to claw a short, miserable life out of the unforgiving sod. Are you such a family? Do your kids dress in gingham and sackcloth and walk around chewing dried prairie grass and playing games with incomprehensible frontier names like Job's Foxtrot and Johnny Fetch the Hoppin' Bean? No, they don't. They're too busy staring slack-jawed at MTV2, memorizing the lyrics to Ludacris songs, and grinding the joints of their thumbs into jelly trying to master the high-speed drive-by shooting in Grand Theft Auto. Your kids don't have time to chew their food. Do you really think they have time for a thoughtful observation of the subtle life lessons you and your husband are trying to teach them? By *example*?

The sad truth is that Mrs. A. O.'s kids are at no time focused on her or her husband with any more rational attention than a mosquito brings to bear on the source of the blood which keeps it alive. I don't choose this analogy casually, by the way. A child may recognize in its parent the source of some elemental needs (clothes, shelter, food, AA batteries) in the same way a mosquito recognizes the flabby wattles under the arm as a source of rich, delicious blood. But do you think the mosquito pauses for a millisecond in its kamikaze descent to consider the middle-aged woman in an unflattering tennis skirt who is attached to the wattles—to appraise her behavior, consider her motives, learn lessons, draw conclusions? If you were within earshot of the comfortable second-floor study in which I am writing this, that sound you would hear would be Mr. Irresponsible whooping with derisive laughter. No, the mosquito is a perfect little machine, designed in toto for the selfish capture of the materials which keep it alive, and untroubled by any form of cognition.

Which brings us back to kids.

Mrs. A. O.'s kids, like all today's children, are so over-whelmed with input that it is a stark impossibility they'd have any brainpower left with which to volitionally observe the behavior of their parents and extract any lessons.[5] For that reason, the lessons must be brought to them. This is why Mr. Irresponsible counsels parents to . . .

....

5. This is not to suggest that your child may not, as its stimulus-dulled eyes swing listlessly from the TV to the Playstation, inadvertently seem to focus on you for a split-second. This is the phenomenon Mr. Irresponsible has named Apparent Contact*, and it is the source of much parental heartbreak.

Make the World Your Manners Lab.

What do I mean by this? Simply that a parent should take every opportunity to draw a child's attention to bad manners as they exist in the wild, and to instruct accordingly. If, for example, you and your kid are in a movie and the squareheaded college junior sitting behind you insists on offering loud, unsolicited comments like . . .

- "Hoo! That guy's crazy!"
- "He went in that door! He went right in that door!"
- "[Repeats onscreen punch line]; hehhehhehheh hehhehhehheh!"
- "Damn, she ran him over with her car! 'Djou see that? *Damn*!"

. . . take this opportunity to offer some gentle instruction in manners to your kid! First, apply one fF of attention-getting force to your child's temple, causing him to turn away from the screen and focus dimly on you. Act quickly, now, because you only have a moment before your child's autonomic nervous system will begin to draw his gaze ineluctably back toward the screen. Reaching into your pocket or handbag, produce one (1) telescoping military crowd-control baton. These are available at police supply and Army surplus stores, or from a wide selection of cranks and loners reachable through the Internet. Extend the baton to its full length and make eye contact with your child as if to say, "Pay attention, now, Jason/Tiffany." Turn in your seat and say to the squarehead, "Would you stop talking?" When the squarehead turns to you, as he inevitably will, and mutters a threat, an obscenity, or both, smile pleasantly and apply the whip end of the baton to the bridge of his nose with a short, decisive downward stroke, adding, "Please." This last part is important, as it reinforces for your child the necessity for politeness in all social interactions. Now sit back, relax, and enjoy the show!

Have Yourself an Irresponsible Little Christmas

Let's take another example. In early 1996 I received this letter, from Mrs. J. C. of Minneapolis:

> I recently took my kids downtown for some last-minute Christmas shopping. I was so saddened to see how rude and out of sorts everyone was. I know the holidays are a time of some pressure for us all, but is there anything I can do to see that my kids aren't affected by others' lack of manners at holiday time?

Consider a shopping trip to a big-city department store at holiday time - the streets fresh with snow, festive banners hung from the streetlamps, mooching Salvation Army volunteers begging for change on every corner. You have brought your children — let's call them "Jason" and "Tifanny" — into the city for a day of shopping, and boy, aren't you regretting that decision now! Jason's blood sugar is dipping into negative numbers, Tiffany is scared of everything she sees, and you're stuck with a towering stack of brightly-wrapped presents which will only fill your in-laws with a puzzled feeling and the urge to scrabble in the tissue paper for a gift receipt. And what, you may be wondering right about now, did those bloodsuckers ever do for you except empty your refrigerator, drain your bar and trample the new lawn you put in this spring to replace the old one they trampled last fall? Nothing, that's what. (See Chapter 5 for more information on "In-Laws: The Gift You Can Never Return.") So you're steaming pretty good as you reach yet one more soulless chain store and heard the kids, who are by this time reeking of sweaty wool and despair and emitting an unattractive whining sound, into the revolving door. A woman with entirely empty arms, carrying not so much as a Kleenex, stands in the door just ahead of you. Spotting you over her shoulder as you enter the revolving door, she stops. And waits. For you to push.

My advice to you is: Shake your head just once, vigorously, to clear the red-tinted fog of murder from your eyes, and recognize that nature has provided you with one more opportunity to instruct your young ones in the practice of good citizenship. What next? Place the packages on the floor. Take your time. You have plenty, because your new friend will wait, and wait, and wait for you to push the door. Research indicates that a person as blindingly inconsiderate as the one you now see before you has extra reservoirs of patience and an imperviousness to the world around her that is almost rhino-like.[6] Clear from your mind the image of Willie Cicci locking a rival gang boss in a revolving door much like this one and executing him with a bullet fired through the glass in *The Godfather*; this is wishful thinking, and it does you no good. Now trigger the "*Hey!*" response through a carefully-applied finger-flick. Are the kids with you? Good. Holding your palms out in front of you, perpendicular to the floor, take as much of a step back as your close quarters will allow, then firmly step forward and *push the door as hard as you can*. Follow through and keep pushing. The key here is to attain enough velocity at the point of impact to propel the door forward at an accelerated rate of speed, catching Ms. I-Can-Wait-All-Day by surprise and clipping her smartly across the Achilles tendons, causing her to stumble for-

....

6. These traits are believed to be seated in a part of the frontal lobe identified by Dr. Danziger of the Blalock Institute as the Rudeness Zone.

ward. Unfortunately for her, your little wedge-shaped section of the revolving door is now a mighty locomotive of righteous wrath, so as she attempts to regain her footing she will be swept *right past* the store's interior and back out onto the freezing, slushy sidewalk, where if there is a God in Heaven she will twist an ankle and fall to the sidewalk in a disheveled heap. Stop the door at this point. Pick up your packages and enter the store, pausing only to shout a cheery "Merry Christmas, Toots!" out toward the sidewalk. The lesson is sure to penetrate the consciousness of even the most overstimulated child: It's holiday time. Be *good*, for goodness' sake.

Human Rudeness: The Lightning Round

I've received many more letters than these on the topic of bad manners, and taken together they represent a rich tapestry of human rudeness. The sheer variety of ways which people find to be rude to one another is breathtaking, and in a way[7] a testament to our powers of invention. Still, a high-volume problem demands a high-volume solution. Herewith, a quick summary of some of the anti-rudeness measures I've suggested to readers over the years.

....

7. A horrible and perverse way.

The guy talking loudly on a cell phone in Starbucks:
Coffee has many fine qualities, not least of which is its
high content of formic, acetic, and propanoic acids. These
are particularly voracious in their destruction of the poly-
mers used in the fabrication of cell phones. Starbucks
stores, tending to be on the small side, place pots of hot
coffee in close proximity to customers. Add to this calcu-
lus the guy ahead of you who holds up the line while regal-
ing a fellow member of the sales staff with details of his
triumphant swing through the St. Paul metroplex.[8] And
you? You have an elbow, possibly two, and weight to shift.
Use them.

**The driver who speeds up and blocks your way when
you signal to merge:** Every gesture has meaning, and the
meaning of this gesture is that the driver really, really wants
to get close to you. So let him! Drop back just enough to let
him pull ahead, then floor it and latch yourself to his rear
bumper, flashing your lights and blowing your horn. Keep
this up for five miles, or until he exits. If stopped by the
police, explain that you're celebrating because Michigan
just made the Final Four. (Carry a selection of Michigan fan
gear—banners, pennants, hand-drawn signs and foam fingers—with you at all times just in case.)

....

8. A quick trick to recognize a salesman on a cell phone: use of the terms "buddy,"
"tee time," "Lexus," "proactive," "honcho," or "mazooma."

The passenger who tilts his airplane seat back into your lap: Science tells us that the recirculated air in airplane cabins contains a high concentration of fleurons, the sub-atomic particle believed to cause rudeness.9 Thus the person who cranks his seat all the way back until he is practically lying in your lap is not volitionally being ill-mannered. Still, he's inconveniencing you, and the easy solution—cranking your seat all the way back—only serves to initiate a pyramid of rudeness that ultimately reaches its apex with the person in the last row of the plane, who is already suffering from his unfortunate prox-imity to the bathroom. No, better to exact your revenge on the person who's directly affecting you. The keys here are stealth and timing. Wait until the dinner service is con-cluded, the movie is over, and the cabin lights have been dimmed. Remove from your carry-on a tube of depilatory cream and a Sharpie.10 Moving quickly and quietly, remove the hair from the top of the person's head. Work as far down toward the collar line as the angle allows. On the

....

9. Also an abnormally high content of amoxium, an enzyme thought to be impli-cated in short-term lowering of standards. This may explain why otherwise dis-criminating people will read anything in the seat-back pocket, eat anything that's put in front of them, and watch any Adam Sandler film, even without headphones, for the duration of long airplane flights.
10. Obviously, a razor would work better here, but Mr. Irresponsible urges you to observe all current airline security regulations.

blank canvas that now presents itself, inscribe the words "I'M A JACKASS" or anything else that seems germane. "But, Mr. Irresponsible," you protest, "that won't do anything to get the guy's head out of my lap." This is true. Sometimes we have to settle for second best, which in this case is the snickers and derisive laughter of strangers. That'll have to do.

The salesperson who ignores you to take a personal phone call: The implication here is that the salesperson's personal life automatically takes precedence over the job for which she is paid a salary. The salesperson is counting on you to passively endorse this theory with your meek silence. But why be passive? Mr. Irresponsible says join in! Lean on the counter, cock an ear, and make yourself a part of the conversation rather than a mere bystander! Here are some suggested all-purpose interjections to get you started:

- "Girl, *whaaaat?*"
- "I'm scared 'a *you!*"
- "Shut *up!*"

Even the most blindingly self-centered person is sure to notice that you've moved right into her conversational living room, settled down, and popped open a Red Bull. At some point she's sure to stop and ask you what you want, if only to shut you up. Don't mistake this for actual interest in you. Remember: it's all about her, not you. But you will, for the moment, have her attention. This should be long enough to get her to ring up your purchase and be on your way.

Parents who let their kids run wild in a restaurant:
This is a tough one. Mr. Irresponsible believes that children are the future, and also that your attitude determines your altitude and that dogs never lie about love. This doesn't mean, however, that I choose to have my concentration shattered just as I'm about to take the first bite of a $38 Maine lobster. (Mr. Irresponsible also believes that you never get back the first bite of a $38 Maine lobster.) There are a time and a place for the banshee shouts of children at play, and that time and place are "not now" and "far away," respectively.

So what's to be done when a young child—let's call the child "Jason" or "Tiffany"—comes rocketing by your banquette, high on juice boxes and Happy Meals, his or her needle-sharp shouts of glee Dopplering past your unwilling eardrums? I'll tell you what's *not* to be done: Don't bother talking to the parents. The parents are useless. They're either exhausted beyond all hope of reason or the sort of New Age chowderheads who would rather saw their own heads in half than stifle little Jason/Tiffany's "creativity" and

....

11. The dependent argument—that a sustained scream and the flinging of brightly colored Fisher-Price doodads across a public space is neither creative nor self-

"self-expression."[11] No, here you must act *in loco parentis*.

Note that injuring the child-rocket is out, as it is frowned upon by both law and custom. The best one can do in this situation is break the child's concentration, as one does with a puppy caught befouling an Oriental rug. So try this: You will have a small arc of time and space during which Jason/Tiffany crosses your field of view. Time this carefully; that arc is as clear and crucial as the launch window for a weather satellite. Let a couple of revolutions go by. Note the precise moment at which the child passes most closely. Get ready. Here he/she comes. Drop your napkin to the floor. Bend to retrieve it. As Jason/Tiffany passes, your mouth should be just at the level of his/her ear. Say clearly but *quietly*, so only the child can hear: "Hey, look! Mommy's dead!"

This should be enough to arrest the child in mid-flight, like a paddleball reaching the length of its rubber leash. Tears may follow. In any event, the running and screaming will stop. Basic instinct will either root the child to the floor (in which case a parent will come retrieve him/her) or propel the child to the parents' table. In either case, you have a respite in which to enjoy your meal.

....

expressive, but rather shows an untrammeled lack of control—will get you exactly nowhere. Don't even try it.

Of course, these are just a few of the many, many ways in which human rudeness may manifest itself. But the basic principles are broadly applicable:

- *Seize* control of the situation.
- *Take* momentum away from the offending party.
- *Turn* their lack of consideration to your own advantage.

In a pinch, remember the simple mnemonic "Seize/Take/Turn," or "STT." Admittedly, this is a bad mnemonic. But what do you want from Mr. Irresponsible, that he should save the world from rudeness *and* take the time to draft your mnemonics for you? That's downright rude.

Chapter

Work

Work: Why?

Quickly now: are you heir to a great family fortune, the kind accumulated by forebears who were much more industrious than you,[12] who piled up huge reserves of spendable cash and died from sheer monkey-brained joy while backstroking through the azure waters off their own South Pacific atoll? Of course you're not. I know this because the über-rich have no need for personal advice books, or for personal advice, or for any kind of advice at all. They have the steely confidence that only vast wealth can confer—the kind that comes from knowing not only that the wolf is not at the door, but also that the wolf would be brought down by armed private security long before it ever reached the door, or would simply die from

....

12. Or unscrupulous. "Much more unscrupulous" also works in this formulation.

exhaustion traveling the several well-manicured miles between the road and the door. (This emotional equilibrium is one of the things that make the very rich feel they are better than other people, which, let's face it, they are.)

The rest of us, meanwhile, need to schlep along in a grubby fashion, piling up enough money to live, if you call that living. (See Chapter 4: "The Magic Beans That Allow Us to Feel Good About Ourselves.") Even Mr. Irresponsible, who has achieved material success undreamed of by the average Joe, has bills to pay: utility bills, lawyer bills, liquor delivery bills, lawyer bills, the rental on his electronic ankle bracelet,[13] lawyer bills, armed private security bills—the list goes on and on.

Seen in this light, it becomes clear that work is an imperative of the only kind more sacred than social or moral imperatives. It is a *lifestyle* imperative, in that it allows us to maintain a high degree of what social science calls the QoC, or Quotient of Comfiness.[14] And it is for this reason that we work: because as humans we *must* work, lest things like satellite TV and $2,600 Sharper

....

13. In any civilized municipality, the county would pick up the tab. This will be the basis of a huge lawsuit to be filed just as soon as my attorneys clear the numerous other huge lawsuits to which I am currently a party.
14. The concept of the QoC achieved mass popularity with the surprise success of Chandra DeVilbiss's best-selling *QoC Workbook* in the mid-1980s. The book allowed readers to figure their own QoCs based on a 120-part questionnaire tallying positive life aspects such as Butteriness, Lack of Shame and Fine Corinthian Leather. DeVilbiss was featured on the cover of *People* magazine, was a frequent guest on

Image massage chairs be tragically unavailable to us. Work is a complicated construct, however, as richly studded with pitfalls and booby traps as a Thanksgiving ham is with cloves.[15] Read on.

Getting the Job: Darwin's First Rule

The awful moment may come at the end of high school, upon graduation from college, or around 30, as it came for Mr. Irresponsible, when a wellspring of lucrative partial-disability checks ran dry: you're going to have to go out and get a job. Wait, it gets worse. Unless the job you seek is so irredeemably awful[16] that no one else is likely to be applying, you will actually have to compete for it. This is a pretty fair definition of "adding insult to injury." Still, once one has cleared the psychological hurdle, there seems little point in going halfway. You are doomed to a state of jobfulness. There it is. And, once your peace is made with the idea, something happens that is both interesting and horrible, like David Blaine:[17] the job

....

the *Larry King* radio show, and even served as host of QoC Masters, a syndicated TV game show which foundered when no one could manage to say the name without giggling. She was later convicted of tax fraud, and reemerged in 2002 as the straight-talking neighbor, Rev. Chandra, on the UPN sitcom *No You Didn't.*
15. Mmm . . . delicious!
16. Some examples: veterinary urologist, freelance telephone-pole creosote applicator, the guy who has to go out and tell people with a straight face that a new Wal-Mart will be good for their communities in the long run.
17. This is true, except for the "interesting" part.

becomes yours. You "own" it, in the way that victims of post-traumatic stress disorder are encouraged to "own" their pain. Now what? Are you going to allow some other applicant to get *your* job? Not likely. In fact, it is your responsibility to your very species to see that he doesn't. It's an evolutionary demand, for who could be better qualified for this job than you are, considering the depth of anti-job feeling that had to be overcome? Is it really possible that this other yokel clawed his way out of a deeper pit of job-related loathing than you did? That he wanted to get up every morning and go to work *less* than you do? No it's not, and therefore you are the single person most supremely qualified.

This was the basis of the psychological spine-stiffening I tried to give Mr. J. McD. of Boston, when he wrote to me in the winter of 2002:

> I've just found out that my best friend and I are going after the same job. Randy is a great guy, he was the best man at my wedding, and he has five kids and supports his parents. You could say he needs the job a lot more than I do. Should I withdraw my application and look somewhere else?

In Mr. McD. we hear a *cri de coeur*. Mr. Irresponsible is only human, and the emotion this plaintive appeal caused to swell in my breast was simple and profound: it made me want to stuff something heavy in the guy's pockets and pitch him off a high bridge. Instead, because giving advice is *my* job and I had at the time no more desire to lose it than anybody else with half a brain, I offered the following counsel, which I expand on here.

It may be helpful to think of competing job applicants the way construction workers think of rocks—as obstacles to be removed by any means necessary. Do you think a demolition contractor gives the slightest thought to the lump of granite that blocks the straight, tidy procession of his chalk line to the horizon? He does not. He reaches for a shovel, and if a shovel fails he reaches for some dynamite, and at the end of the day he looks at the spot where the offending block of matter used to sit and thinks, *Good.* This is how you must think about anybody who stands between you and the job you have settled for. If, as in the case of Mr. McD., the block/person is an old friend, so much the better. Imagine if the demolition contractor in our little story knew precisely where the stress lines existed in the stubborn, intractable face of the granite, and could split the block in half with one well-placed blow of a hammer instead of 20 and go have a meatball sandwich. Isn't that an outcome to be encouraged? Doesn't the job get done earlier in the day, with less wasted effort, freeing the contractor to have some lunch and return to work feeling rested and strong?

Similarly, let's suppose that years of familiarity have given you some acquaintance with Randy's stress lines. If you know, for example, that Randy bursts into tears at the mere mention of his childhood dog, a sheltie named Mac who was killed at the age of 14 months by a runaway ice cream truck, doesn't it seem wasteful not to use that information? He told you because *he wanted you to know*. It was late, you were drunk, he was in a confessional frame of mind, and if he ended the conversation by wrapping you in a bear hug and whimpering "I've never told anybody that, buddy, thanks," well, that's not nearly the same thing as saying "Look, don't ever use this to make me crack open like a piñata in a stressful situation," is it? Don't you owe Randy the courtesy of not reading into his statement something he never thought he meant?

Now the question becomes one of simple methodology. Given this insider knowledge by whatever higher power you believe in, how best to use it? Alacrity is the key here. What you need to do is get into the interview room first. Once inside, the interviewer will be expecting a few moments of small talk. Here's your chance! Tell him you ran into your friend Randy in the waiting room, and that he's a great guy with many fine qualities. For instance, he loves dogs. Hey, ask him to tell you the story about his dog Mac and the ice cream truck! It's a scream! The seed of Randy's destruction planted, proceed with your interview and say no more about him. Then leave the interview room with a cheery wave to Randy, head home, and wait for the phone to ring. In the meantime, if you choose, you may have a meatball sandwich. You've earned it, after all. You blasted Randy out of the unforgiving soil and cleared the path to full employment. Somewhere up above, Darwin is smiling down on you. You got the job.

Office Life: Be a Racehorse

Most of us will never know the blood-thumping rush of military combat, but just about all of us will experience the savage intricacies of interoffice warfare.[18] The two are remarkably similar, except that almost no one gets their limbs blown off answering sales calls at an office supply company. One other key difference: the military has basic training. What preparation does the average salaryman have for the lifetime he'll spend behind a desk, in a cubicle, under

....

18. With two exceptions: the über-rich, as previously noted (God, how I ~~hate envy despise~~ admire them!) and anyone lucky enough to scratch out a living as a dispenser of personal advice.

soul-leaching fluorescent light? Not much. That's where Mr. Irresponsible steps in. Consider this letter from Mr. D. B. of Fresno, which came my way in the winter of 1992:

> I've been at my job for 11 years and have seen three new people hired under me, all of whom have since been promoted over me. I'm starting to think I may never get the respect I deserve at this job. Can you help?

I could, although the help I offered at the time— which was to twist my voice up into a whiny Cockney and wheedle "Please, Mr. Scrooge, I've been your clerk these 14 years and all I ask is a ha'penny bonus, because after all, Mr. Scrooge, *it's Christmas*"—may not have been exactly what Mr. D. B. was after. So let's look at this one again.

The basic scenario here is all too familiar, and without knowing the particulars I can guess that Mr. D. B. is that most unfortunate of office-dwellers, the Guy Everyone Counts On. Late with a project? Drop it on D. B.'s desk. Shorthanded at holiday time? Good old D. B. will fill in. Don't have time to show the new guy the ropes? Hand him off to D. B. If there's a job too small to be dumped into D. B.'s lap, you're going to need electron microscopy to find it. Now, you can call this diligence, call it work ethic, or call it what you will, but Mr. D. B. has dealt himself a losing hand here. Any boss with half a brain will recognize a vested interest in keeping Mr. D. B. right where he is.[19]

So what's to be done if, like Mr. D. B., you find yourself the office workhorse? The first thing is to remember what happens to workhorses—they end their days swaybacked and exhausted, smelly and spent. Now consider what happens to racehorses, those gloriously high-strung and unreliable speed machines—they end up at stud, eating delicious grasses and having their coats combed by teenage girls. Thus, Mr. Irresponsible's First Law of Office Politics: *Be a racehorse.*

What do I mean by this? Be flighty, demanding, unpredictable. (Your officemates will find this fascinating, and you mysteriously alluring.) Decline work (or "scratch," as I think of it) when conditions are unfavorable. (Do you think a racehorse loses the esteem of its colleagues, or its chances for professional advancement, when its trainer declines to race it on a muddy track? No, it simply heads back to the stall and grabs some more feed.) And when job performance is inevitable, as it sometimes is, perform

....

19. A variety of management studies, including the landmark Terwilliger Project at Yale Business School, have found that a solid plurality of bosses do indeed have half a brain.

with flash and blinding speed. (Results are fine, of course, but ultimately less impressive than the way the wind ruffles through your mane.)

In a few years the actual, measurable quality of your work will have blended seamlessly with an overall picture of style and grace, and the two will have become indistinguishable from each another. And, if the history of business has taught us anything, it's that advancement depends on looking good. Besides, there will certainly have been a Mr. D. B. around to pick up the slack. Years from now, as you relax in the executive lounge, give him a thought. Maybe even drop down and see him one of these days, if you can clear the time from your schedule. Or not. After all, you're pretty busy.

Being the Boss

Careful readers may detect an anti-authoritarian strain in Mr. Irresponsible, to which I can only say, "Who died and made you boss?"[20] In fact, I am not reflexively anti-boss. I am a boss myself, and Debbie would tell you that I treat her fairly and openly, with perfect trust in her loyalty and discretion. Or she would tell you that if she weren't signatory to the most brutally restrictive confidentiality agree-

....

20. Thanks. I'll be here all week.

ment ever devised by the mind of man.[21] This represents a good encapsulation of my feelings about bosshood: *Trust, but indemnify*. Let's look at a letter from Ms. T. E. of Milwaukee, which I received in the fall of 1989:

> I've just been promoted. I worked hard for the promotion and think I deserve it. The problem is, a number of people who used to be my colleagues now report to me, and I hate to say it, but some of them are taking advantage. How should I handle what's becoming a very uncomfortable situation?

In my haste to draft my original reply,[22] I neglected to make an essential point. The phrase "A very uncomfortable situation" is the key to this letter. Uncomfortable for whom? Both sides, presumably. But Ms. T. E. is failing to take something important into account here, and that is what might be called the Comfort Bump, which she received as part of her pro-

....

21. My lawyer assures me it makes the documents signed by former employees of Tom Cruise and Nicole Kidman look like "a Where's Waldo placemat." I don't know exactly what this means, but I take his point.

22. *Mercy! Advantage is being taken! Heavens, someone call the job police, or an advice columnist who cares! I think that biddy Ann Landers is available!* ("Mr. Irresponsible's Bad Advice" newspaper column, October 23, 1989).

29

motion. It is the least understood but perhaps the most significant perquisite of bosshood. In effect, it is the right conferred on her to feel comfortable when her underlings do not, and to do so utterly without remorse.[23] She's new in the job, so the slip can be forgiven. But she must learn to think of the Comfort Bump as a part of her overall compensation package, no less important than salary or benefits, and act accordingly.

How best to put this attitude into action? The key is an unswerving confidence in the rightness of your position, no matter how wrong you may actually be. In fact, the wronger you are, the righter you must act. Only by refusing at all costs to acknowledge error can you as a boss maintain a high level of personal comfort. Let's say, just to pick a silly example, that you have instituted a new policy requiring all employees to wear cheesehead hats on the Fridays before Packer home games. You further direct that all employees must wear their cheesehead hats at all times while on company property, and you've

....

23. There is an allied phenomenon, the Remorse Differential, which is the degree of difference between how remorseful bosses and employees feel when something goes wrong in the workplace. Experienced bosses aspire to a 100 percent RD—that is, a total lack of shame on their own parts, coupled with a complete offloading of it to those who work under them. Only the very best bosses ever achieve this sort of perfection, but it is the great ones who try, always try.

instructed Skip the garage attendant to deny entrance to anyone who isn't wearing a cheesehead hat. This means that your employees are donning their cheesehead hats at home and driving to work in them, their peripheral vision is being obscured, and accidents are being caused. Within the office, as the day goes on, fistfights are starting to erupt between employees who wear their cheesehead hats with the pointy end facing forward and those who wear them with the rind end facing forward. A small fire breaks out on the 14th floor after a member of the rind group shoves a member of the pointy group into the Xerox machine, which skids across the floor and upends a can of Vanilla Coke, spattering soda into an electrical outlet. There are scattered reports of mob violence on the sixth through ninth floors as break-away factions of Eagles fans suddenly appear in cheesesteak hats. By 5:00 the building is surrounded by SWAT teams and firefighters, but Skip is doggedly denying them entrance because "their hats don't look right." A delegation is dispatched from City Hall to meet with you and broker a compromise. They are delivered to the helipad on the roof and make their way to your office, where you are by now ensconced like Col. Kurtz on a huge batik cushion,

dressed in camo gear and a cheesehead hat and surrounded by a small cadre of heavily-armed temps
who remain loyal to you and the Packers. The mayor
pleads with you to lift the cheesehead-hat policy long
enough for the women and children and Bob from
Accounting, whose asthma is starting to act up pretty badly, to get safely off the grounds. If you don't, he
says, he'll have no choice but to call the governor and
have the building stormed by the National Guard.
"This has to end now," the mayor says. "If it doesn't,
people will die."

"Sorry," you say. "My hands are tied. It's Cheesehead
Friday."

"But why?" the mayor pleads.

"Because," you say calmly, "that's our policy."

Do you see? You have set policy and seen it imple-
mented. This is your job. Whatever happens after that,
whether it's a bad financial quarter or an armed siege ending in fatalities and the reduction of company HQ to
blackened, smoking rubble, is beyond your control. To
have bent would have taken you out of your comfort zone,
and, worse still, made you appear weak before your
employees. And then you would have been finished. So
remember these basic principles of bosshood: Admit
nothing. Bend never. And, when the time comes to

demonstrate strength, resolve, and bossly dignity, put on your cheesehead hat and go out there and earn their respect.

Chapter

Friendship

Friends: Nature's Way of Reminding Us How Very, Very Good It Is to Be Alone Once in a Goddamn While

Ah, friendship! What would we do without friends? I don't know, but I do know this: we would do it alone, in blessed silence, without a leeching cacophony of hangers-on to trouble our days and pluck at our shirttails, bleating of ancient childhood memories and the $1,100 they allege to have lent us six years ago for a toupee that most certainly did not turn out to be 100 percent undetectable, no matter what the ads claimed.

I don't mean to suggest by this that friendship is without worth. I only mean to suggest that it isn't wholly worth the trouble. For make no mistake—friends are trouble. With friendship comes responsibility, and with responsibility come entanglements . . . strangling, choking entanglements, weaving about your windpipe like the unraveling strands of a cheap toupee. How much better it is to sail through life as a free agent, picking and choosing the interactions one wishes to have on the basis of factors more compelling than, say, the accident of history that places one person in the back seat of a burning taxi and another on the sidewalk. And if the latter sees fit to turn up years later, protesting in a baffled voice, "But I *pulled you from a burning taxicab*. I *saved your life*. How could you sleep with my wife?", isn't it valid to ask what possible connection there could be between the events of a single, long-ago, smoke-choked Tuesday and the mysterious ways of the human heart? Isn't it just confusing to conflate the two? You bet it is.

The way to stave off that confusion is to keep your eye on what's in front of you. What happened yesterday, be it the alphabetic accident that seats one schoolchild next to another through 12 years of education or the quirk of chaos theory that leads one person to, yes, *pull me from a burning taxicab and save my life*, for God's sake, is history.[24] What happens today is the only thing we can control. And today Mr. Irresponsible chooses to triage his interactions not on the basis of those chance encounters but on the simple, highly

....

24. It seems worth noting that one wouldn't even have been in the flaming, melting back seat of the taxi that day if a stray spark from the driver's Newport 100 hadn't ignited the flammable tendrils of a certain poorly fabricated toupee. Enough said.

quantifiable basis of a fundamental question: "So. What can you do for me?"

With this clarifying rule in mind, let's look at some ways to simplify the often complex process of human friendship.

The Lifestyle Lie: Truth Is Overrated

In the summer of 1995 I received this letter from Mr. P. S. of Kearney, N.J.:

> I frequently find myself with social obligations that I agreed to some time before, and when the time comes around I just don't want to do them anymore. Is there some way out of these obligations without hurting people's feelings?

There certainly is. Mr. Irresponsible recommends the judicious use of the lifestyle lie.

It was my mentor, Prof. Max Gewirtzel of the Berlininstitut der Lernensachen, who is believed to have coined the term "lifestyle lie."[25] (It has also been

....

25. A personal word, if I may, on the late Prof. Gewirtzel. The student body had a great fondness for the diminutive academician, for his quick smile and engaging lecture style and the way he would, after one or two lagers, tip over when pushed,

called "the lie of facilitation," although I am uncon-
vinced that there is such a word as "facilitation." If
there is, there shouldn't be.) In a nutshell, the lifestyle
lie is one that ameliorates a complicated social interaction, easing the way toward an irritation-free existence.[26] Practiced with proper care, the lifestyle lie is a
simple technique that can reduce social dreariness by
up to 67 percent.

Say an elderly friend of your parents comes to
town. Let's call this specimen "Morty." Let's postulate
further that he's visiting his son, a dull-witted semipro-
fessional screenwriter who has never once, when you
have had the misfortune to run into him around town,
failed to bend your ear with interminable accounts of

....

then bob back to an upright position like an inflatable "Push Me" clown. Indeed, in
his younger days at the Berlininstitut he was one of the more popular members of
the faculty, and was even voted Keymeister at the 1949 Faculty Dance, a position of
high honor and respect. Had he not become enmeshed in a rather tawdry contro-
versy involving an underage "research assistant," he might have been able to live out
his days at the Berlininstitut—teaching, moderating lively discussions among his
students, and engaging also in more private pleasures, such as sipping dandelion
tea in the afternoons and tending to his beloved collection of souvenir pencils. But
he did, and died in disgrace instead. As Gewirtzel's friend and confidant Hans
Linzner put it, in moving remarks delivered at the tiny scholar's funeral: *"Gut, was
sind Sie gehend zu tun."* ("Well, what are you gonna do.")

26. For the person lobbing up the lie, of course, as opposed to the party on the
receiving end. Indeed, the recipient of a lifestyle lie will almost certainly find himself more burdened with social obligation than before. This is consistent with the
notion that social obligation can be neither created nor destroyed, only offloaded to
others. For more on this, see Prof. Gewirtzel's seminal 1963 study, "I Owe You, You
Owe Me: Breaking the Deadly Cycle of Dinner-Party Invitations."

his failures in Hollywood. Let's call this one "Morty Jr."[27] Uh oh, it's double trouble! You are, let's say, relaxing at home on a Tuesday evening. Your phone rings. "Kid," comes the wheezy voice on the other end, all Chesterfield Kings and bottom-shelf Scotch, "I'm at Morty Jr.'s. We wanna see you."

The ancient fight-or-flight response kicks in. A bracing jolt of adrenaline floods your system. The gears of the lifestyle lie engage with a smooth, barely audible *click. System on. Obtain information.* Because it is information that is your ally in the preparation of the lifestyle lie.

"Morty!" you cry, feigning good cheer. "How long are you in town for?"

"Just till Thursday." *Thursday. That's two dinners from now if he counts tonight. Which he certainly will, because he's just inconsiderate enough to propose a last-minute meeting. Two breakfasts, unless he's taking an early flight. Which he probably is, because they're cheaper. Call it one breakfast. One lunch. A possible coffee.* All this takes less than a second.

....

27. Morty Jr., as is typical of the delusional artist-wannabe, fails to take any personal responsibility for his warp-speed descent to the bottom of the professional ladder. There is only one tactic with a chance of penetrating this carapace of obliviousness, which behavioral science tells us has all the tensile strength of Kevlar. That is to grab Morty Jr. by the shoulders, shake him vigorously, and scream directly into his face: "Wake up! Did you really think a musical adaptation of 'Shoah' was going to put butts in seats?" This may or may not get through to the subject, but is widely acknowledged by social psychologists to be "fun."

"Oh, no," you say. "I'm on a deadline." *Danger: He might be on a noon flight. He'd have to check in by 11. Better build in some wiggle room.* "Thursday afternoon. Gotta beg off."

"Come on," comes the rhino-like reply. "A cup of coffee."

"Didn't you know?" you say. "Gave it up."[28]

"How about lunch?"

"I'm on that no-lunch diet."

"Dinner?"

"Atkins."

"How about a salad?" *A skid! Steer into it!*

"Diverticulosis." *Nice. Now park that baby.* "Jeez, Morty, it's a damn shame. When are you coming back?"

"I don't know. The thing is, kid, my doctor says I only have—"

"Great! You be sure to give me a call, now."

And quickly, before he can rally, hang up. Morty will be left with a narcotizing sense-memory of pleasantness on your part, like the faint whiff of popcorn that hangs in the air after the fear and misery of Cirque du Soleil have

....

28. The beauty of this approach is that for a second it puts Morty on the defensive, as if there were truly some way he could have been expected to know that you'd given up coffee—via ESP, perhaps, or a notice on the Times Square Jumbotron. This is absurd, of course, but the momentary flicker of reproach in your voice helps keep him off-balance.

subsided. And you'll be off the hook to spend your next few days as you choose. You can even spend them working, as you told Morty you would. A lifestyle lie that morphs into eventual truth is nothing to be ashamed of. There's no reason to be dogmatic about these things.

Getting Through Parties Alive

In the early spring of 2001 I received this note from Mr. G. B. of Parsons, Ala.:

> I've been invited to a party hosted by some friends of my friend Gina. Now Gina can't go and I've already RSVPed. So it looks like I won't know anybody there, and this makes me nervous. What should I do?

As I recall, my first reaction when I received this letter was to wipe my hands on my shirtfront, so convinced was I that Mr. G. B. had actually contrived to impregnate the paper with some of his pale, sweaty milquetoastiness. You know how some people give you the creeps and you don't know why? This wasn't like that. Mr. G. B. gave me the creeps and I knew precisely why: it was the palpable air of desperation, and the unmistakable aura of a guy who lives in a studio apartment with a larger-than-usual complement of cats. The only mystery about it was how he ever got this Gina to look his way. I have some theories on this, and they involve a trip to Tijuana and the purchase of substances that aren't normally sold over the counter in the U.S. And now, gosh, what do you know: *Gina can't go*. I may be stepping out on a limb here, but let me suggest that the interval between the invitation and Gina's sudden withdrawal more or less corresponded to the time it takes those substances to decay and leach from the bloodstream. But perhaps I've said too much, and after all the poor guy wrote to me in the first place for help. So help him I did, immediately after which I took the longest, hottest shower of my life.

Let's consider just what we talk about when we talk about parties. They are, first of all, a purely human construct. The concept of the party is almost entirely unknown in the animal kingdom, which is just one of the many, many things that make animals more fun to hang out with than humans. The sole exception is a ritual observed on the veldt of southern Africa, in which several dozen hyenas stand around an open grassy area, moodily lapping at brackish water, chattering away in a desultory fashion, and then arbitrarily turning on one of their own and killing him. This has been likened by animal behaviorists to the basic pattern of the annual office Christmas party, only with less remorse the day after.

Can there be any real rationale for the human party? At least in the above scenario the guests get to eat, which is not always the case at human parties, unless you count a tray of Wheat Thins passed at light speed around 11:30 P.M. The reasons usually offered for planning a party seem pitifully flimsy when held up to the light:

- "It'd be fun to get the gang together."
- "We never get to see each other outside the office."
- "Let's blow off some steam!"

To which one need only answer, in turn:

- No, it'd be fun to split the gang apart, widely, and permanently if at all possible, using industrial power tools.
- The only thing I want to see outside the office is the big, wide world.
- If you want to blow off some steam, go skeet shooting. Just leave me out of it.

Yet people insist on wedging their acquaintances into poorly-ventilated living rooms, forcing them into awkward small talk and ritually starving them with an undersupply of refreshments which, were it the menu of any self-respecting Turkish prison, would be flagged in a heartbeat by Amnesty International.

Clearly, changes are in order. Gandhi advised that "we

must be the change we wish to see in the world." It is this Gandhian principle which guides my behavior on those infrequent occasions when I am forced to attend parties, and which I passed on to Mr. G. B., and upon which I expand now. What's needed here is a comprehensive approach to party survival. I can offer it in three simple steps:

1. Find a place in a corner. This provides psychological security as well as cutting down the sightlines you'll be forced to maintain. Secure a drink for your left hand and an appetizer for your right; this will forestall the partygoer who leaps gazelle-like from behind a potted plant to grab your hands in greeting and physically prevent you from getting away. Avoid ice in your glass, as it will dilute the drink and force you to leave your safe harbor for another. Consider the purchase of lifelike acrylic sushi from a restaurant-supply store to serve as your "appetizer." Thus armed, you will to all outward appearances seem to be simply pausing in the corner for a drink and a nosh. Remain there at all costs.

2. Adopt a pleasant, neutral expression. Fix your eyes on the middle distance, or a spot just to the left or right of the door. I practice an ancient technique the Greeks called "≢τηε Ευε Τηατ

Λοοκσ ανδ Σεεμσ το Σεε< βθτ Δοεσ Νοτ Σεε≢" ("The Eye That Looks and Seems to See, but Does Not See"), in which my gaze appears to focus, move about the room, and register movement, although in fact my eyes are totally unfocused and all I actually see is a restful wash of muted colors. It took years to learn and in all likelihood contributed to the non-stop, blinding headaches from which I suffered between 1987 and 1993. But it was worth it, and I recommend it. All I'm saying is, preparation is good.

3. Using your peripheral vision, watch for the approach of fellow partygoers. If someone begins to come your way—let's call him "Dougie," because there are no circumstances under which you want to get cornered by somebody named "Dougie"—lift your chin and waggle your eyebrows as if greeting a friend across the room. If Dougie continues his approach, start across the room toward your invisible friend. Wait for a crestfallen Dougie to change course. Return to your corner. Repeat step 1.

Using these three basic techniques, it is possible to get through what I call the "PoEP"® *(Period of Empty Politeness)* and not have to exchange so much as a word with anyone.

But, you ask, what happens if you see someone headed your way whose obliviousness is so rhino-like that even these careful defensive maneuvers seem likely to fail—a sort of Über-Dougie? That's an easy one: know where the fire alarms are and how they work. Thus armed, it will be almost as if Gandhi himself is standing in the corner next to you, giving you an enthusiastic thumbs-up for putting change into practice. He may also be eyeing your sushi surreptitiously, but there isn't anything you can do about that.

Meeting New People: Who's Disposable?

In the late spring of 2000 I received this letter from Mr. J. B. of Las Vegas:

> I've just moved here from Durango, Colo., and am having trouble meeting people. I haven't made very many friends at all. Can you help?

I could, and did, although the advice I gave Mr. J. B. at the time may not have been what he was expecting.[29] I'm pleased to be able to revisit it now.

....

29. *My advice to you is in two parts. One: look up the word "puling" in any good dictionary. Two: stop doing it. Coworkers find it off-putting, casual acquaintances will run flat-out in the opposite direction, and it will kill you stone dead with women. Or men for that matter, if you swing that way, and it's all the same to me. What makes you think I care about your sex life, anyway? Why does every yutz with a pen think I give a hoot about his or her sexual proclivities? I swear, I am so sick of answering questions about sex! Sex, sex, sex! It's all I ever hear about anymore! Why don't I get*

The misapprehension under which Mr. J. B. seems to be laboring is that meeting new people is a matter of quantity. This is a popular fallacy; social success is a *quality*-based equation. That is, success isn't a matter of how many new people one meets when, say, arriving in a new city. If it were, the long-haul bus driver who delivers anonymous loners and drifters to Manhattan would be the toast of Broadway, and the Port Authority would be the Stork Club. I think we all know how far from the truth that is. No, social success is a matter of *which* people one meets, and to what extent they can help further one's goals. Remember our old friend Charles Darwin? If Darwin—or "Chuck," as I like to think of him—were here today, in the comfortable study where Mr. Irresponsible is drafting these words, well, he would probably berate me for thinking of him as "Chuck," as he was a notoriously cranky old coot. But he wouldn't say I'm wrong.[30]

To the sentimental objection that human relationships can't possibly be measured like spoonfuls of sugar,

....

questions about anything but sex anymore? It's like people are obsessed with it nowadays! It's all they can talk about! They turn perfectly innocent questions into insane rants about sex! Well, I've had it! ("Mr. Irresponsible's Bad Advice" newspaper column, May 22, 2000). In retrospect, the spring of 2000 was a rough time for Mr. Irresponsible.

30. He would probably wonder what he was doing in the comfortable study of a split-level ranch house in the year 2005, as he died in Kent in 1882. I'd have Debbie fix him a sandwich while I tried to explain. Debbie makes a Croque Monsieur that has been known to induce signs of the Rapture.

let me offer this: What sort of spoonful are we talking about? A teaspoon? A tablespoon? One of those big giant spoons they use to stir huge pots of pudding in the military? Ha! They must hold pounds and pounds of sugar! So who's Mr. Accurate now, smart guy?[31] In fact, the value of new people can actually be quantified with a high degree of precision, using Dr. Febiger's famous formula:

$$FVQ = (SAT \cdot 10yAI)x / (FC + 1)$$

... where a subject's SAT scores are multiplied by 10-year average income, the resulting figure is raised to a power equal to the number of college classmates who sit on the boards of major corporations, and the whole she-bang is divided by the number of extant felony convictions plus 1. The result, the Friendship Value Quotient, has been shown to predict the degree to which a given acquaintance may do a person some good with accuracy of over 90 percent.

"But Mr. Irresponsible," you say, a look of confusion darkening your features, "am I supposed to get all that information about every new person I meet? And how do I do that without offending them, anyway?" I retort: *Please.* Do you think Sgt. York or Audie Murphy or whoever the hell it was worried about offending the Germans or

....

31. Game, set, and match.

the Japanese or the Swedes when he was charging up that hill, or through that trench, in the Marianas or the Maginot Line or whatever it was? Exactly. And neither should you.[32]

Although the more timorous of you may resort to third-party solutions like Google or private detectives, it is perfectly acceptable to tackle the problem head on. Let's say you're newly arrived in town, and are introduced to a friend of a friend. "Nice to meet you," this person begins. "How long have you b—" Stop him right there. Tell him you may be new in town but you're not *new in town*, if he knows what you mean,[33] and you haven't got time for pleasantries. Whip out a small notebook. (I always carry one with me for just this purpose. Some new people are offended at the sight of it. I figure their discomfiture is a small price to pay for my peace of mind in knowing I've got the facts down right.)

Act quickly now. In a commanding tone, bark out, "SATs?" If your party evinces confusion, take this as a black mark against him. (I like to make an actual black mark in my notebook at moments like this. It's dramatic, and says you mean business.) Say it again, a bit more

....

32. If these names don't mean anything to you, you should learn a little something about history, my friend.
33. Even if he doesn't, and I'm not sure I do either, the phrase's tough-guy rhythm is enough to stop most people in their tracks.

forcefully: "Your *SAT scores*." If he now claims he doesn't remember, it's black mark number two, and this is really starting to be a bad day for the poor guy. In quick order snap out the remaining questions: "Ten-year average income? Number of college classmates on the boards of major corporations? Felony convictions?" If the subject continues to hesitate, encourage him with the words "Chop-chop!" By this time, however, if you haven't got the information you need to make an accurate computation of FVQ, cut bait and move on. It's a good rule of thumb that most people you don't know have something to hide. Whether it's a stray assault pinch or just an abnormally low score on the English side, can you really take that chance? Mr. Irresponsible doesn't think so. Neither should you.

Chapter

Money

The Magic Beans That Allow Us to Feel Good About Ourselves

It was fashionable during the '60s (a decade which still makes Mr. Irresponsible shudder) to say that money isn't real. This may be true, but poverty sure is. Let's say, just for kicks, that I grant you a thesis: money is a mere theoretical construct used by the power class to quantify the degree of its chokehold on the workers. I'd still like to see you get past the drive-up window at Taco Bell without some. Try telling the kid behind the glass that you "don't believe" people "need money" to "buy things." I bet you'd end up staring down the business end of a cheap handgun. And when I won that bet, which I would, I too would demand a cash payout, not the proffer of some handwoven leather goods in barter, or a patchouli-scented hug or a sincere wish to have a nice day. I don't *need* your wish to have a nice day, Princess Sunshine. Do you know why? Because I can provide my own nice day very adequately, thank you, with the money that I earn by my labor. This is the greatness of the capitalist system: I don't need to depend on anybody else, especially some flyspecked throwback to the Summer of Love, to guarantee my own comforts. And the more I become successful, the more comfortable I am able to be.

Note that I didn't say "the harder I work" just then. This is because it's naïve to extrapolate an expectation of material success from hard work. If there were a causal connection between hard work and material success, teachers would live like rajahs and pretty-boy teenage TV stars would starve to death. If hard work equaled material success, do you think I could have taken the advance for this book, which is in actuality little more than a slapdash repurposing of half-baked bromides I didn't even really think through the first time, and plunk it down on a weekend place in Palm Springs? Fat chance. So, the next time you're tempted to float away to Starrytown on the wings of some adolescent notion that, gee whiz, if you just *knuckle down* and *work hard* you're *sure* to get rich, do Mr. Irresponsible a little favor, will you? Get on the bus and tell the driver to take you to Sunrise Way, just off San Rafael Road, because there's a very wealthy man who needs you to squeegee his pool tiles. I'll be waiting for you.

Making It

I'll be discussing three aspects of money in this chapter, and of the three this is the one that professional economists agree is the least fun. Making money demands adaptability and technique, as I tried to tell Mr. J. L. of Albuquerque when he wrote to me in the winter of 1992:

> I've been working at my current job for almost nine years, and I'm barely making enough to get by. I'd like to ask my boss for a raise, but I'm scared of him and there are a lot of people in the office who could take over my job. What should I do?

Yikes, it's hard to believe Mr. J. L. hasn't skyrocketed straight to Easy Street with that kind of can-do attitude, isn't it? Let me expand a bit on my original advice to him, even as I stifle the urge to stuff him in a sack.

Nobody likes going to work (see Chapter 2: "Work: Why?"). Even people who claim to love their jobs secretly wish for a life of wealthy indolence. Yet they get up every morning about 9-ish and go off to the office and work. [34] How do they do this? I have no idea. If I had to get up

....

34.   I may be a little hazy on the details here, as I am happily self-employed and get up whenever I feel like it.

every morning about 9-ish and go off to some office park I'd commit seppuku. But I can suggest a theory, and it was a version of this advice that I offered the unfortunate Mr. J. L.: people's loathing for work is overcome by what the German social scientist Prof. Gert Wildner called their *Sache-wünschen Sie*, or "Things-desire."[35] Now, this process is not instinctive, nor does it come easily, particularly in cold climates where it frequently bumps up against what might be called the *Bleiben-in-ein-warm-bequem-Bett-auf-ein-kalt-Februar-Morgen-wünschen Sie*, or "Staying-in-a-warm-comfy-bed-on-a-cold-February-morning-desire." Mr. Irresponsible is here to help. Perhaps a little story will show us the way.

Many years ago, before I achieved the material success I enjoy today (and I enjoy it very much indeed), I had a summer job unloading trucks in the warehouse of a mail-order pet-supply company. The hows and whys of it aren't important, except to say that my father believed it would "toughen me up" to get some experience of "the real world." This from a man who wept at *Finian's Rainbow*, but never mind—there I was. I haven't checked with astrophysicists, because Debbie has started refusing to make phone calls for me, but in retrospect it seems

....

35. Even the most arcane concept livens up when it has a silly German name, doesn't it?

possible that time actually slowed to a crawl that summer. The other guys on the receiving crew were my only companions, and I'd say something like "I wonder what ever happened to them" except that I really don't care, and besides, if any of them managed to get out of the indentured servitude in which they lived and get other jobs, I'll eat my desk, and believe me, this is saying something because I have a *big* desk.

So there I was, a 19-year-old with a dream, which consisted of digging a tunnel out of the warehouse, disappearing into the night, and smothering my father while he slept. But—and this is the point—I still had a job to do. How did I do it?

Psychiatrists like the ones I was sent to after that summer, when I just couldn't seem to stop making colorfully specific threats against my father's life, call it "creative dissociation." As far as I'm concerned, this is just a fancy-schmancy name for some good old-fashioned capital-I Imagination![36] When I looked at, say, Vinnie, I didn't see the dock foreman with the sprouty tufts of neck hair and the deskful of pornography; I saw right *through* Vinnie to what the summer with Vinnie was going to get me: a brand-new Sony TC-651 sound-on-sound reel-to-reel tape

....

36. And not a "borderline sociopathic disorder," whatever that's supposed to mean, Dr. Pincus, you hack.

deck with a four-channel playback head and auto-reverse. When I looked at one more grimy 18-wheeler backing slowly up to the dock, its yawning door revealing yet more pallets of Nutro's Nature Max dog food and shrink-wrapped Scratch-King cat towers, I saw none of it. Instead, my mind's eye painted a picture of huge, bass-rattling quadraphonic speakers. Over there, that wasn't that loafer Carl, sneaking another snooze in the freight elevator; it was the complete *The Who Live at Leeds*, on first-generation Ampex studio-quality tape. The phenomenon was very much like the one undergone by a hungry Wile E. Coyote when he would look at the Road Runner and see a giant roast turkey, complete with paper sleeve doilies over the drumsticks.

Narcotized thusly (and also in some other ways),[37] I managed to get through the summer. All it took was a laser-like focus on the results of my labor, and the ability to, in a correspondingly focused and intense fashion, ignore the actual work before me. Thus my advice on making money: money itself is useless unless considered in the crisp, beautiful light of the things it can get us. If life has dealt you the kind of hand by which you are compelled to actually go out and work for your money, don't

....

37. Thanks, Carl!

whine and complain and sulk, at least not initially. (You may want to do so later on, but that's later on.) Follow Mr. Irresponsible's simple three-part advice: *hallucinate, hallucinate, hallucinate*. And, if you see my father, tell him I have something for him.

Spending It

What is it about money that makes otherwise appealing people, people who in every other respect may have dash and flair and a sense of *la dolce vita* about them, turn into drab little men with glasses? In the fall of 2000 I received this letter from Mr. T. K. of Santa Ana, Calif.:[38]

> I've inherited some money from a distant relative and my friends are advising me to invest it. Some of them are saying I should find a nice no-load mutual fund, and others are telling me I should look at municipal bonds or T-bills. What do you think?

I advised Mr. T. K. that I have a small difference of opinion with his friends. Instead of investing, I believe

....

38. I have no way of knowing whether Mr. T.K. has dash, flair, and a sense of *la dolce vita* about him, nor for that matter chic, panache, pizzazz, cleverness, savvy, quickness, "the knack," "the goods," or "the stuff." I'm just making a point.

that he should spend all his money as fast as he can, and then get some new friends.[39] Only in spending, and doing it quickly and recklessly, like a sailor in the sex bazaars of Thailand, can he be true to what I like to think of as the Spirit of Money™.[40] For never doubt that money has a life force. It is this force that we feel the absence of so keenly when we are broke—that comforting hand on the shoulder, that loving voice that whispers, "I am Money, and I love you."[41]

Mr. T. K.'s error is that he is not listening to that voice. He is listening instead to the cabal of the investor, which is really just a offshoot of the "Money isn't real" crowd we discussed earlier. The cabal of the investor would have you believe that money is a mere instrument, a theoretical thing to be used in the pursuit of *more* money. Do you see the fallacy here? If one uses one's money only in the blind, unreasoning pursuit of more money, when does one get to do what one is truly supposed to do with money, which is enjoy it? When does one get to exchange one's shekels for velvety crème brûlée, hand-sewn suits, foolishly fast Italian sports cars? What

....

39. In fact, if Mr. Irresponsible's experience is any guide, once he starts throwing it around he'll have all the new friends he can handle.
40. Mr. Irresponsible does not recommend literally spending all one's money in the sex bazaars of Thailand. He has a friend who did this once, and had to wire home to Debbie for the funds to get back.
41. It sounds a little like James Earl Jones.

do we work for, anyway, if it isn't these things and the color they provide to our otherwise pedestrian lives? Do we work for a "sound financial footing" or "something put by for a rainy day"? Oooh, stop, Mastroianni, I'm breathless with the romance of it all![42]

To further compound Mr. T. K.'s error, he is talking about investing the very best and most desirable kind of money, *inherited* money. This is like taking a very good New York Strip and pounding it flat for use in chicken-fried steak. Inherited money is a gift from the gods and, if you doubt that the gods can work through, say, your elderly Aunt Estelle from Frostbite Falls whom you haven't seen since you were 11 and she pinched your cheek so hard it left a mark, then you haven't been paying enough attention to the gods' prankish sense of humor. One *must* take inherited money and blow it foolishly, exuberantly, grandly, for it is in so doing that we best honor the memory of whatever nice old lady it was who left it to us. Do you think she intended for you to stash it in a certificate of deposit at 2.2 percent per annum? Do you think that's what she wants to look down from heaven and see? No, she wants to see you racing Formula 1 cars at Daytona.

....

42. The same principle applies to charity, in which perfectly good money is applied to abstractions like "ending world hunger" or "curing disease." Money doesn't do well with abstraction. Money does well with goods and services.

She wants to see you running with the bulls at Pamplona. She wants to see you hang-gliding at Moab. All these things are gloriously life-affirming, and like everything else that's life-affirming they take a good deal of cash. Don't let that sweet old dead lady down, now.

So, to summarize: Investment is bad. Charitable donation is bad. Money is good, inherited money is better, and reckless spending is downright fabulous. If one follows these few simple guidelines, one can have a good time in life. But what, I hear you ask, happens when you spend all your money? The answer is self-evident: it's time to start spending someone else's. We'll look at that in the next section.

Losing It

Saint Augustine famously wrote that it is "better to have loved and lost, than to have never loved at all." This snappy little sentiment has survived for roughly 1,600 years because, let's face it, when you want advice on your love life, who better to turn to than one of the fathers of the Church?

Far be it from me to suggest that the bishop of Hippo had his spiritual head up his ecclesiastical butt when he wrote this. In fact, I agree with him. What I disagree with is the extension of the sentiment to other areas of life. For example, it is most definitely *not* better to have had money and lost it than to have never had it all. In fact, it is way worse, as I tried to tell Mr. D. G. of Manhattan, Kans., in July 1995:

> I was a poor kid, and I'm strug-
> gling now as a husband and
> father to pay the bills. I don't
> want a free ride, but sometimes
> I wish things were a little bit
> easier on me and my family. Is
> there any advice you can give
> me to help me handle these feel-
> ings of frustration?

In retrospect, my original advice may have been a tad brusque.[43] Allow me to elaborate:

Science tells us that life is entropic, that it tends toward deterioration. So, for heaven's sake, what is Mr. D. G. whining about? He was poor, and he *still is*. Where's the loss of ground? In fact, I'd argue that Mr. D. G. is one of the lucky ones, because by starting out poor and staying that way he has managed to resist the elemental patterns of decay that govern life on Earth. Think about it: he has

....

43. *Oh, please. Tell you what, why don't you go sell some platelets and use the proceeds to buy a clue?* ("Mr. Irresponsible's Bad Advice" newspaper column, July 17, 1995).

managed to heroically hold his ground in the face of unimaginable forces. And, by golly, that ain't just whistling Dixie. It's an *achievement*, something to pass on to the kids and the grandkids in lieu of an inheritance.

Now let's talk about the truly unfortunate: people who have accumulated great personal wealth and then lost it. These are certainly the saddest of God's creatures. They have been allowed to glimpse Valhalla—Valhalla in this case being a land of nice hotels and shiny black town cars—only to have their day passes revoked. They have been lifted up and brought down low again, and if that doesn't give you the bends then I don't know what does.[44]

So what can we do to anesthetize the pain of losing money? Sadly, most of the really good anesthetics cost money, which is an unfortunate Catch-22. But Mr. Irresponsible has a strategy to offer, and it can be encapsulated in three words: *Be a leech*.

Leeches have historically gotten a bad rap. *Hirudo medicinalis*, the medicinal leech, is regaining favor in medical quarters, where it is used to relieve pressure and restore circulation in grafted tissue. It's also believed that there are antibiotic qualities to leech saliva, which is at

....

44. No. Wait. Not the bends. What's the one where you get nosebleeds at high altitudes? Altitude sickness, that's what I meant. Oh, screw it; I'll fix it in the second printing.

once the ickiest and most significant discovery to impact reconstructive medicine in many years. In other words, the spunky little bloodsucker is actually good for us! Similarly, I believe, people who have lost wealth can perform a valuable prophylactic service for acquaintances who haven't been so stricken. By attaching themselves to these parties they can actually bleed off the excess money that leads to bad behavior. They can, at the same time, do a little something to salve their own psychic trauma. It's a true symbiosis.

How to do this? There are many ways. Become one of those hometown hangers-on who trail around after the pop singers on MTV, drinking on their tabs and signing their names to limo bills. (Your local chamber of commerce can help you identify celebrities who hail from your area.) Business acquaintances are frequently looking to fill out a foursome; hang out at the pro shop and keep an ear cocked for familiar voices, and you'll never have to pay a greens fee again. Take to standing around in front of expensive steakhouses, checking your watch, and looking steamed; when friends from your old circle arrive, which they inevitably will, tell them sheepishly your date stood you up. Then feint toward the taxi stand and wait for that dinner invitation to come your way!

Using these few simple techniques, you should be

able to dull the sting of lost prosperity, keep yourself fed and amused, and help your better-heeled friends avoid the excesses of extreme wealth. It's a win-win situation. Just keep one thing in mind: If you happen to see Mr. Irresponsible pull up to that steakhouse, tell your story walking. I'm no Jessica Simpson, and I *will* call the cops on your mooching ass.

Chapter

Family

Even Luggage Gets Thrown Away Eventually

Mr. Irresponsible's official bio is many pages long and contains accolades enough to shame the most shameless celebrity.[45] But it contains no references to family. I've been asked why that is, and I can reveal it now: I have no family. They were killed many years ago in a freak accident involving steam and industrial solvents. I've been alone in the world ever since. Hardly a day goes by that I don't think of them.

This isn't strictly true. The truth is, my family is alive and doing fine. I mean, I assume they are. Someplace in the Midwest, I think, although I'm not really sure.[46] But do you see what just happened? For one second, an involuntary trace of pity arced its way across your neurotrans-

....

45. Sharon Stone.
47. I know it's somewhere they eat beer brats.

mitters. This ancient, vestigial impulse is related to the pack structure of early man, which sought to ensure security in numbers. The more relatives, the less the chance one might be carried off unnoticed by a predator. The hominid who was unlucky enough to stand alone on the vast plain presented a tempting target, and thus became an object of pity for other packs, which watched from the sheltering obscurity of nearby grasses.

What makes you just want to smack human evolution with a stick is this: it's been millions of years since this paradigm held true, and yet there was that little tickle of prehistoric pity, shoving its way into your primitive forebrain like an unwanted guest at an after-bris coffee. If evolution had half the wit of the social sciences, it would realize that it's been quite a while since a solitary human stood defenseless on the grassy plain. A solitary human on the grassy plain these days is most likely to have wandered off from a luxury safari tour, and if he kneels and places his head to the ground in the ancient gesture of supplication he will probably be able to hear the rumble of the air-conditioned Land Rover which has tracked him by GPS and is on its way to pick him up and take him back to the Four Seasons.

And where is his family? In all likelihood, back in the States, getting up and going to work and barely registering that they have a pack member unaccounted for. The closest thing that remains to the instinctive howl of a frightened, lonely animal is the postcard that says "Greeting from Kenya, Wish You Were Her" (with a picture of a buxom young African woman on the front). This is promptly discarded when it reaches the family back home, as I think we can all agree it should be.

So it seems only logical that we reevaluate the whole notion of family ties.

Siblings: One of Us Isn't Going to Get Out of Here Alive

Pity the only child! The only child never knows the rewards of brotherhood, the joys of sisterhood—of struggling for a parent's love, of constantly looking over your shoulder to see if you're losing ground, of fighting to carve out your own identity in the shadow of a sibling who's older (and thus better equipped to face the world) or younger (and thus cuter and more defenseless, leading to increased attention). So pity, *pity* the only chi—Oh. Wait. I don't mean "Pity the only child." I mean "Boy, does the only child have it made or what?"[47]

This was the gist of the advice I gave Ms. A. C. of

....

47. Sorry. Mr. Irresponsible gets all mixed up sometimes.

Kansas City, Mo., who wrote in the summer of 1994:

> My brother Frank and I have
> always gotten along fairly well.
> Recently my Aunt Jeannie died
> and left some money to our
> mother, her sister, to be split
> between Frank and me. She did-
> n't specify how it was to be
> divided, tho. Mom wants to give
> Frank more because he's older
> and also because he has a fami-
> ly to support (I'm single). I
> think the money should be divid-
> ed evenly. Frank disagrees, and
> things are starting to get tense
> between us. What do you think
> Mom should do?

Here we have a textbook example of the cruel joke which is siblinghood. Lashed at the hip to a stranger with whom we may have nothing in common except an unasked-for genetic closeness, we are forced to compete. And not just for jelly sandwiches and footie pajamas, either, but for life essentials like respect and affection. Is it any wonder so many of us grow up with a distrustful nature and a tendency to sleep with one eye open?

So I think now, as I did in the summer of 1994, that Mom should do this: She should place a motherly hand on each of her kids, smiling warmly as only a mother can, and then knock their heads sharply together, causing a sound like two coconuts being struck.[48] Then she should take the money and go to the Golden Door for a few days. If there's any dough left when she gets back, she should construct an enclosure out of old scrap metal, lock the kids inside, and tell them to settle it with a Texas Death Match. This might not technically solve the problem, but it seems likely to give the neighbors some laughs.

Mr. Irresponsible speaks with some authority on this subject. I have a sister, who for the purposes of this discussion we will call Jackie Irresponsible. As I mentioned earlier, she is to the best of my knowledge living somewhere in the Midwest, where she is married to a guy named Mort (or Mart, or Mert, I think) who sells the caustic chemicals used to clean aluminum siding. At least I think that's what he does. Last time I saw them all, at a cousin's wedding, this Mort/Mart person spent a few minutes of my time muttering drunkenly about how he was "doing some hush-hush work for the government." This

....

48. Mrs. A. should receive a bonus rap on the noggin for the overly cute way she spells the word "though." Mr. Irresponsible has never understood this habit. Are the extra two seconds it would take to append the letters "u-g-h" really so precious to Mrs. A.? Apparently not, because she seems to have whole luxurious oodles of time to kvetch to me about the shabby way her mother is treating her. If Mr. Irresponsible were running things—and don't think he hasn't thought about it—people who are this casual with spelling and syntax would be beaten with sticks.

may have even been true, if by "work for the government" he meant peddling cleaner to the next town over so they could power-wash the shed where they store the rock salt, but never mind.

The point is, I have a sister named Jackie. Jackie volunteers at her children's school, drives for Meals on Wheels, donates a fixed percentage of her income to charity, has her car inspected regularly, crosses only at the green, calls her elders "sir" and "ma'am," and sorts her recyclables. Do you see my point? How is it possible that a just God or a rational universe, whichever way you swing on that question, actually saddles a person like me with a relation like Jackie? I mean, I have fine qualities to burn, and Jackie . . . well, Jackie is a drag, a dweeb, a Poindexter. How much irreplaceable life force does the average person burn on living such a sibling down, or keeping up with one, or simply keeping track of where she presently lives, when—let's be honest—an accident of birth is the only thing the two have in common?

So why not do this: lose the dead weight at your earliest opportunity and place all that psychic energy where it can do some good, i.e., on advancing your own fortunes. Do as Mr. Irresponsible did on that blustery morning 23 or possibly 24 years ago, when he left home to make his way in the world. Shake your sibling's hand and say, "So long.

See you at Mom's funeral, maybe." Then set out vigorously toward your destiny, shorn of the relation you never asked for, just as if you'd gotten a very short, very stylish haircut, and can feel the breeze of the future rustling for the first time against your neck. *Aaah*.

In-Laws: The Gift You Can Never Return

It was Aristophanes, I believe, who first observed that "in the capering of Fools there is much wisdom."[49] Consider the Mother-in-Law Joke, which has been definitively characterized as one of the three pillars of modern comedy.[50] Is there anything more basic and familiar in the entire lexicon of laughter? Indeed, the Mother-in-Law Joke is so ubiquitous that it's been rendered almost meaningless.[51] And yet there exists in it, as in all great comedy, a saving shred of truth.

The underlying cry of pain in the Mother-in-Law Joke is that the victim has been saddled with a carping

....

49. My notes indicate that he observed this in March 1966, so it's entirely possible it wasn't Aristophanes at all. It may have been some old drunk I met at the Friars Club.

50. The other two: "What's Up With Airline Food" and "White People Are So Uptight That. . . ." See *I Laff, You Laff, We Laff: The Building Blocks of Funny* by Shecky "Morty" Gunzelman (University of Michigan Press, 1972).

51. Except for the one about the guy who picked up his mother-in-law at the airport last night; *boy*, those airport lounges are dark! That one never fails to get big laughs around my house.

relation whom he never specifically invited into his life, who hates him not for anything he's done but for what he *is*—i.e., the person who married her daughter. Of course, this dynamic applies equally to females and the mothers of their husbands. (Man, does it ever.) Consider this letter from Mrs. D. G. of Louisville, which came my way in the fall of 1996:

> I've tried everything I can to get my mother-in-law to like me. I've invited her into my home, asked her along on family vacations (at our expense), cooked her countless meals, called to check in on her several times a week, and endured a long series of passive-aggressive insults. This has gone on for the whole nine years I've been married to my husband, Frank, and I'm just about at my wit's end. Can you help?

I could have, if there weren't laws in Kentucky against hiring ex--Special Forces guys to disappear peo-

....

52. Not that I know any. Nor am I aware of a Del Taco run by an ex-CIA wet team in a strip mall just outside of New Albany.

ple.[52] Short of that, my advice to Mrs. D. G. was more theoretical, and I expand it upon it here.

The key to dealing with troublesome in-laws, which is almost a tautology, is to remember that they are *the accidental byproducts* of adult relationships, not an integral part thereof. And what's to be done with byproducts? Look at the example provided by American industry. Do you think business wastes one minute of time trying to get, say, lignins, which are a byproduct of the process by which paper is produced from wood chips, to *like* it? Do you think the board of Amalgamated Pulp and Paper sits in emergency sessions wringing its hands about how mean lignins are to it, and how little its lignins appreciate everything it's done for them? Doubtful. No, industry teaches us that there are but two things we can do with byproducts, and neither involves cooking them a meal or calling them twice a week to make sure they're okay. We can simply dispose of them, burying them deep in the Nevada desert or dumping them into nearby lakes or streams, but once again, in the case of humans, local laws tend to preclude this sort of thing. Better to repurpose the byproducts of your marriage into something potentially useful, as in the process that renders useful plastics from those unloved lignins, or makes low-grade cat treats out of otherwise worthless cow parts. Some suggestions:

An alarm clock. If you have an in-law who insists on calling you every day to ask why you don't have children yet (or why you haven't "given me a grandchild yet," as if the child were an overdue wedding gift), let slip that you rarely get to sleep in past 6:30 A.M. Then toss that old Westclox and wait for your personalized 6:30 wakeup call!

A TV listings service. Can't remember what night *The West Wing* is on? In-laws watch hour after hour of television, if only so they can carp about it the next day. Call your in-law and ask if she's ever seen that show about the people who work for the president. "It used to be so good," will come the instant reply. "But I watched it last night, and I swear, I don't know what they did to it." Bingo: Wednesdays!

A living history of your spouse. Can't remember when your wife started crumpling up her napkin and dropping it on her plate after dinner, or when your husband started balling up his socks and tossing them in a corner at night? Just let your in-law observe the behavior in question once, and she'll thoughtfully help you narrow the timeline: "I just know he didn't do that before he married you."

An all-purpose compendium of human knowledge, from cooking to gardening. Unsure about the proper way to season a pot roast, or when to put your roses to bed for the winter? Simply let your in-law watch, then wait for the inevitable "That's not how you do it. What were you, raised by bears? *This* is how you do it. Oh, for heaven's sake, let me."

A constant, grinding check on your self-esteem. Ipso facto.

Children and Dogs: A Comparison

Isn't it time to ditch the outmoded notion that procreation is necessary for the survival of the species? I mean, have you read the papers lately? We're either going to immolate ourselves in one fantastic act of geopolitical hubris or be expunged en masse in some wrongheaded cycle of tribal savagery and reprisal. If neither of those happens, it seems likely we'll at least wake up some morning to find that the Earth's orbit is degrading and we're plummeting into the sun and, man, won't that be a bummer of a day. With all this as backdrop, do you really think it matters in the long term whether we continue to crank out youngsters? The argument is narcissistic in the extreme. So please, let's take it off the table, as I urged Ms. A. L. of Philadelphia when she wrote to me in the summer of 1994:

> My husband Lenny and I are trying to decide if we want to start a family. I want to and he

> isn't sure. Not to be corny about
> it, but I feel like it's the reason
> we were put on Earth. What can
> I do to convince Lenny I'm
> right?

As I told Ms. A. L.: Honey, there must be better ways to use your dwindling time as a sentient being on Earth (see above). May I suggest just one? Get a dog.

To the inevitable argument that a dog is no substitute for a child, let me reply clearly: This is correct. Dogs are superior to children in every way—they're loyal (but not blindly so), affectionate (but don't demand emotional ties), and aesthetic (at least in the larger breeds). And they trump children in one way above all: Children force you to participate in the narratives of their lives, which are of necessity sharply delimited, while dogs allow you to construct theirs. To a dog, you are a god; to a child, a stooge.[53]

Consider the father out for a morning walk with his small daughter. "Daddy!" she cries, noticing her feet as if for the first time, "I have flip-flops!" "You sure do, honey,"

....

53. There is a further, or "bonus," reason to forgo parenthood: a prospective parent who declines the honor immediately inherits her unborn offspring's lifetime allotment of fossil fuels, a figure reckoned by independent research to average 116 cross-country road trips per spawn, at highway speed, with air-conditioning blasting. This explains the high numbers of childless persons observed driving giant SUVs half a block to pick up the laundry. Mr. Irresponsible always offers these citizens an enthusiastic thumbs-up as they tool by on their huge tires.

he says. This exchange will be repeated, with minor variations, on the order of six dozen times before lunch. Each and every time, the father will have to *hear* the statement, *evaluate it* for content, *reject* it as meaningless, *stifle* that rejection, and *construct* a responsive-sounding but meaningless reply. Studies have shown that the mental effort wasted by this process is stupendous, on the order of some 73 trillion brain-hours per year in America alone.[54] Even when it becomes more or less automatic, as it does for most parents within weeks of the time their child acquires speech, it's exhausting. It's this that explains why parents of young children invariably exhibit the pale sheen and gray pallor of wax paper.

Now consider the guy out for a walk with his dog. The dog bounds picturesquely off behind a tree and emerges with a stick clutched in her jaws, and what appears to be a guileless smile. *Come on*, the dog seems to say. *Chuck that stick. You know you want to chuck it. If you just chuck that stick, I swear to God I will think you are the finest person who ever lived.* "Okay, Mojo, fine," the guy says. "I'll throw the stick for you. Give it here."

....

54. Dr. Emil Glauber of the Salzburg Institute argues persuasively that this is why the decline of America's industrial might has corresponded roughly with the latter years of the postwar baby boom. See "The Sleepiest Generation," *Commentary* magazine, April 1979.

The dog does. The guy throws it. The dog brings the stick back. The process is repeated anywhere from two to eight thousand times, depending on the breed of dog and whether the owner has plans for the rest of the day. The transaction is apparently a simple one. But look at what's passed between the man and the dog: The dog has expressed an inchoate wish, to have the stick thrown. The owner, functioning as a sort of all-powerful screen-writer,[55] has drafted for the dog a piece of unspoken dialogue that is clear, sincere, and rich with meaning. He may even have in his head, as I do with my wolfhounds Hans and Betty, some idea of how the dog would sound were he actually able to speak.[56] Both owner and dog emerge from the transaction satisfied, with no false emotion expended and no brainpower wasted (especially on the dog's part), and as an added bonus the healthy, ruddy glow of a few minutes' exercise.

The moral seems clear. There are probably many reasons why we "were put on Earth," in Mrs. A. L.'s shopworn formulation, and maybe they include some form of godly volition, and maybe they don't, and maybe they

....

55. Which is surely the first time those two words have ever appeared in such close proximity.

56. Hans sounds something like the actor Maximilian Schell. Betty, the more assertive of the two, sounds like a 15-year-old suburban girl. Debbie tells me her Schnauzer, Mr. Whippy, sounds something like the cartoon dog Astro from *The Jetsons*, which I regard as evidence of a lack of imagination on her part.

include natural biochemical processes, and maybe they don't. Theologians and scientists will debate this endlessly, which is one reason you never want to take a long car trip with a theologian and a scientist. But this much is a mortal lock: Want to sleepwalk through your days, wasting your intellect and gradually counting down to Armageddon? Be Mr. Irresponsible's guest, and breed your brains out. Want to communicate simply and meaningfully with another living thing, get some exercise, and go home happy? Think about a Labrador.

Chapter

Love

The Thing We Do Because We Can, and Also Because We're Sheep

For some, romance is Paris in the '20s. Birds twitter; the river babbles; there is the distant hint of music in the air. For others, it is Kuwait in 1991—obscure, smoky-dark, and choked with a killing confusion. Mr. Irresponsible takes no side in this debate.[57] My role here is, rather, to explicate some of the complicated social transactions love makes necessary. For it is when we are in love that we are most naked, emotionally speaking. Also literally speaking, with

....

57. Except to say this: I would rather uncoil my own intestines and plug them into a portable generator than marry again. The 16 months of my marriage were a kind of living, breathing hell, the faceless face of Evil given form and substance, followed by a period of emotional combat so soul-wracking that it made the Inquisition look like Summer Crazee Daze in the Wisconsin Dells. When it was all over I had no home, I had made rich a man for whom the term "shyster" would be an upgrade, and the woman who pledged to stand beside me in sickness and in health was in fact standing eight thousand miles away, on the Amalfi Coast, with a water-ski instructor 19 years my junior. (I was later told his name was "Rolf.") Given the choice between a repeat of my marriage and a cocktail composed of equal parts sarin and goat's blood, I would reach for the cocktail so fast that bystanders would actually feel a small, discrete rush of wind. But, you know, you do what you want.

any luck at all. Getting emotionally naked is like getting literally naked in one key respect: there are some people who just shouldn't. It's those people I speak to now.

Dating, and How to Survive It

In August 2002 I received this letter from Ms. A. L. of San Francisco:

> I've gone out with Steve a few times and we always have fun, but now he's calling me all the time and wants me to stop seeing other people. I'm just not sure I'm ready to get so serious with one guy. What should I do?

Well, it's too late to do the first thing you should have done, which was time travel back to 1966 and direct this letter to *16 Magazine*. Hey, maybe you could have gotten Davy Jones's autograph while you were back there, and, oh, I don't know, found a way to warn President Johnson that Vietnam was, like, a total quagmire that would scar our national psyche for generations to come and junk!

But I digress.

Ms. A. L. makes a common error here: she assumes that dating is about fun. This is not true. Dating is deadly serious. It is a transaction, a strategic exchange of information, a mechanism to determine compatibility between two humans. It is a chess match and an auto-da-fé rolled into one. Sound scary? You bet! "But, Mr. Irresponsible," you say, "all I wanted to do was go have a sandwich someplace and maybe see a movie." Then do yourself a favor: order in from Boston Market and see what's on pay-per-view. You'll have a better time.

So how do we survive the dating years? It's a cruel irony that we find ourselves dating during just those times in our lives when we are most unfit and prone to blunders: as teenagers (acne-riddled), in our 20s (emotionally adrift), and as recent divorcés (walking wounded). If this isn't proof that there's a spiteful intelligence behind the ebb and flow of human lives, then I give up. Still, there are things we can do to increase our chances of getting through the dating ritual alive.

1. Abandon any romantic notions about dating being a quest to find one's soul mate. In truth, it's more like applying for a home equity loan. There are risks to be managed, terms to be arranged, and a potential for disastrous consequences if things don't work out. So it's best to view your date not with romantic intentions, or even (to be strict about it) with friendly feelings. It's best to view her as someone with the capability to destroy your life. Be skeptical, even suspicious. Challenge every assertion. If she says, for example, that "I just love onion rings, don't you?" answer evenly: "No. No, I don't. And I don't believe that you do, either." This will keep her on her toes, and get the evening off to a safe start.

2. Be extremely wary of "small talk." Information is power, even when it seems innocuous. For example, if your date asks where you grew up, nod pleasantly for a moment or two and then scream "WHO SENT YOU? TALK!" Use your own past against you? An amateur mistake, and one she won't make again.

3. Keep in mind that we all have a limited capacity for new information, and there are better uses for it than the mundane details of a stranger's life story. So, if you're trapped on a first date and the person across from you insists on launching into her bio, stop her. Do it like this: "Stop." If she looks puzzled, simply explain that you don't care about the time she came *this close* to the Olympic trials in the long jump. Do it politely, as there's no reason to be rude. In the long run, even she will see that it's more important you reserve your precious RAM for something that actually matters to you.

4. Most important of all, whatever you do, don't fall for the old flapdoodle about dating being a "search for intimacy." Intimacy is wrong and frightening and bad. You do not want intimacy. You do not want to murmur your most secret thoughts to another person. Why have you spent a lifetime accumulating secrets, anyway, which are really just the emotional savings accounts we pay into from our youngest years—saving a bit here, a scrap there, to tide us over through the rough times. Why? To reveal them to someone else? Someone with whom your buddy Stan fixed you up over beers at the Wursthaus, for crying out loud, promising you she's "real nice for someone her size"? Here, let's play a little word game. What are secrets? Are they:

    A) Public

    B) Freely available

    C) Widely disseminated

    D) Openly distributed

    or

    E) *Secret*?

Correct answer: E. That's why they call them secrets. Are we clear on this now? Offering them up to someone you barely know is like signing over the family nest egg to the first grifter who blows into town and dangles something shiny in front of you. And I can tell you from personal experience that's a mistake.[58]

These rules may sound harsh or even unfair, but I assure you they're not. If everyone in the world would observe these guidelines there would be no heartbreak, no misunderstood intentions, no conversations containing the phrase "I really love you as a friend." The trick, of course, is getting everyone in the world to play along. I have some plans about how to do that. And, no, you can't know what they are. They're secret.

Meeting the Parents

In the late summer of 1999 I received this letter from Mr. J. Z. of Tucson:

> My girlfriend and I have been dating for about a year, and it's getting serious. Now she wants to take me home at Thanksgiving to meet her parents. I'm pretty nervous about it. Any advice?

....

58. It turns out that genuine platinum is rarely shiny. Who knew?

Yes, and it's fairly simple: *Be a different person.*

Let me explain. Your girlfriend and your girlfriend's parents have entirely different expectations of you. She expects you to be a confidant; they want you to be unfamiliar with her secrets, lest you use them against her. She wants you to be a sounding board; they want that role for themselves. She wants you to be a lover, and they want you to be a eunuch. Do you see? In every respect that matters, your girlfriend's expectations of you and her parents' expectations of you are not only entirely different, but wholly contradictory, perfectly self-negating. Which leaves you with a choice: Whose expectations do you want to live up to? Your girlfriend's, if you have a brain in your head. Thus it is imperative—indeed, it is virtually a test of your love for her—that you smile, shake hands, and *show the parents what they want to see* before the clock runs down on the holidays and you can go home and resume your real life.

What does this mean? While in the parents' orbit you must present to them exactly, and only, what they expect to see in their daughter's boyfriend. If it makes it any easier for you, try to remember that their mistrust isn't personal. They'd feel this way about any man their daughter brought home, and no doubt have, since the girl was old enough to start being interested in boys. Indeed, when the parents look at you it's unlikely they see a person there at all, but rather an amalgamation of every one of those unlucky previous males. This may explain the distant, unfocused, vaguely angry look in her father's eyes when he answers the door on your arrival. He's placing you in the context of every other boy he's ever met, including the boy he himself used to be, and what he knows about boys is causing him to seriously consider splitting your face open with a cleaver right there on the doorstep. So you must do your best to convince him and your girlfriend's mother that you are the only male in the history of male humans who presents no discernible threat to their daughter's well-being.

The best way to do this is to employ what I call the Eddie Haskell Paradigm®, after the ingratiating, supremely sexless neighbor kid on *Leave It to Beaver*. Ask yourself before every interaction: "What would Eddie Haskell do?" When you do this, and this is the secret, you tap into the stereotype of the unrisky male that is hardwired into all of us from years of popular culture. And don't worry—it's in there, even in people too young to have ever seen the program. Like a needle sinking deep into a vein, you will be mainlining right into a buried source of cultural comfort, and releasing the good, warming heroin of parental expectations subverted.[59]

Begin right away, right there on the doorstep. As the

....

59. Kids: This is a metaphor. Don't do drugs.

father opens the door, for example, pump his hand vigorously and leap into a lengthy, detailed explanation of the route you took to get there. "*Wellllll*, we jumped on the 10 and took it straight to Peck Road, don't you know, only *this one here* wanted to get on the 605 and do that crazy loop and I told her, sugar, don't you know that just adds a half hour to the trip, plus it's coming on rush hour? Anyhoo, we made it in 55 minutes flat and that doesn't count the time we stopped to gas up and grab some nachos, does it, pumpkin?" Believe me, dads eat this kind of thing up like it's pie. Keep going now: Call him "sir" and tell him you're "pleased as punch" to be there.[60] When you meet your girlfriend's mother, pretend you think she's your girlfriend's sister. Call her "young lady" and tell her she's "pretty as a picture." If at all possible, bring a honey-glazed ham and some carnations.

If you effect this transformation right, the parents will quickly decide that you're an idiot. This is exactly what you want. There isn't a parent alive who wouldn't rather have her child date an idiot than a flesh-and-blood male. Thus convinced, they'll settle into their comfort zone and remain there for the duration of the visit. You

....

60. A warning: You will sound like a member of Up with People when you do this. Prepare your girlfriend for the apparent transformation, so she doesn't think you suffered a personality-altering aneurysm during the drive.

may even find that you enjoy acting the part. If not, you can always have angry sex in the car on the way home. And happy holidays from Mr. Irresponsible!

"Should You Marry Me?"

The old leering cliché about marriage vs. cohabitation— "Why buy the cow when you can get the milk for free? Heh-heh-heh"—is wrongheaded in at least two respects. One: "Get the milk for free" is another way of saying "Steal the milk." Two, and this is more to the point, and also less rigidly moralistic: it fails to take into account the wishes of the cow. I mean, nobody ever asks the cow to weigh in. Does the cow even *want* to be rid of the milk? Don't misunderstand; I don't personally care what the cow wants. My interest in cows runs more to their taste-enhancing fat content than any hint of volition which may stray accidentally across their minds. Why, in a world where we started worrying about what the cows wanted, there would be no such thing as a tenderloin and the Las Vegas Strip would be covered with Kentucky bluegrass.[61] "Ruminating" and "emitting methane" would be Olympic events. If cows had their way C-SPAN would be filled with endless discussions of cud-chewing and the benefits of

....

61. This isn't a bad idea, but never mind.

multiple stomachs—of whether, say, the reticulum really is all that when compared even-up with the abomasum.[62] What a world this would be if the cows were in charge!

Hmm. Mr. Irresponsible seems to have wandered rather far afield here.

The point is, there are a lot better ways to decide on something as important as marriage than on the basis of something you hear from a Shriner named Al. Consider the question posed to me by Ms. H. L. in the spring of 2002:

> My live-in boyfriend of six years has asked me to marry him. I love him and we have a great relationship, but I'm still a little nervous about taking this big step. What if it changes things between us? Do you think it will?

My original answer was fine as far as it went, but lacked a certain specificity.[63] Let me expand on it now.

The traditional question, "Will you marry me?" has a certain stately ring to it. It's the stuff of old movies and

....

62. This isn't a bad idea either, but never mind.
63. *Maybe. I don't know. What am I supposed to be now, Mr. Future Guy? Hey, look at me, everybody, I'm Mr. Future Guy! I fly to work on a jetpack!* ("Mr. Irresponsible's Bad Advice" newspaper column, April 11, 2002).

Cole Porter songs and a million gauzy images of bended knees and moonlight. Too bad it's the wrong question. It implies, and for that matter demands, a binary answer: Will you or won't you? Yes or no? How many people have yes-or-noed themselves into lives of misery because they were flattened by the overwhelming cultural weight of that question? It's the Midnight Special of questions, and when it shines its light on you, you either freeze on the tracks or leap out of the way, and in neither case have you made an informed decision.

The right question is: "*Should* you marry me?" This takes the equation out of that binary realm of action and places it where it belongs, smack-dab in the realm of cognition. Now we can look at things in the bright light of pure self-interest, and, baby, that's where Mr. Irresponsible eats.

So picture the scene. You're Ms. H. L. Your fiancé— let's call him Harold, because it's a silly name—has actually dropped to one knee and popped the question . . . the *right* question. "Ms. H. L.," he says, and, okay, it's a little creepy that he calls you that, so there's one strike against him right there. "I love you very much and I can't imagine my life without you. Should you marry me?" Now we got ourselves a ballgame.

"Well, Harold," you begin, "I don't know. On the one hand you're a nice guy and you have good teeth, and that's important because I am *not* waking up some night 40 years from now to hear you sucking on your bridgework in the dark. That's just not gonna happen." Harold may well have a confused look on his face at this point. That's his problem. You're just getting started. "On the other hand, there's your family. Your mother hates me and I'm not so crazy about her either.[64] That's 40 years of little digs and disapproving glances and, I don't know, just thinking about it makes me tired." Harold may be furtively flexing his bent knee by this time, maybe sneaking a glance at his watch. "Oh, get up, for heaven's sake; we're gonna be here a while. You do have stiff joints. Possible arthritis down the line. Not good."

And so on. Compile a mental checklist as you go, or, for that matter, an actual checklist. Borrow a pencil and paper from Harold if you need to. If he doesn't have pencil and paper, dock him a point or two. By the end of the conversation you should have a pretty clear idea of what to do. And if Harold is standing there blinking rapidly, holding out a Tiffany's box with a baffled expression that says "So do you want the ring or not?" well, so be it. To recap: This is one of the most important decisions you'll ever make, and it's pure shortsightedness

....

64. See Chapter 5, "In-Laws: The Gift You Can Never Return."

not to take all the available information into account. And if Harold doesn't understand that, dock him another point or two.

Chapter

Death

God to Us: Shut *Up*, Already

There are as many ways to regard death as there are kinds of human experience. Clearly, this is too many. "But," I hear you asking, "can we really say how many ways there should be to regard death?" Short answer: "Yes. Two." There should be two ways to regard death. This isn't rocket science, people. It's death, and there are but two ways to think about it, and they are determined in the only way anybody ever really determines anything: by how it affects you personally. Let's try this simple, fun test! Did you like the person who died? Then death has taken them from you, your life is a poorer thing, and therefore death is bad. Did you dislike the person? Then death has extracted a thorn from your paw, and in this case death is good. It's a binary equation.[65]

....

65. *Aha! you say. There are millions of people who die every year about whom one knows nothing, and how is one to feel about that?* Let me pause here to clear my throat in a dismissive fashion, mock you for your arch use of the term "one," and reply. The deaths you're talking about exist in the realm of abstraction, a realm for

Of course, moral ambiguity, which Prof. Giancarlo Polpettini of the University of Perugia once memorably described as *"il singolo uomo sgradevole che ottiene ha messo vicino voi al partito del pranzo di vita"* ("the creepy single guy who gets seated next to you at the dinner party of life") intrudes. We can see this in the uncomfortable euphemisms people employ when they talk about death, which are really just linguistic tricks to forestall the kind of on/off, good/bad judgments I've sketched above. We say that people have "passed away," "passed on," or simply "passed," as if they were only in an unseemly hurry to get to the Jersey Shore for the weekend and we've pulled to the side of the road to let them speed ahead. We say they've "faded away," "answered the last call," "cashed in their chips," "taken the big sleep," "flipped all the cards," "gone to work in the Post Office," "polished the pumpkin," "tumble-dried the tuna." All of these evasions can be avoided if you consider the deaths of other human beings in the warm, clarifying light of unrepentant self-interest. Here are a few examples, in handy table form. Feel free to print this table out, lami-

....

which Mr. Irresponsible has little use. In a real sense—i.e., real to me—those millions of people who die each year without having made my acquaintance can be said to have never existed. I'm not disapproving of them, you understand. I'm just saying they are as relevant to me as other purely theoretical constructs, like "military justice" or "Christian love" or "Belgium."

nate it, and carry it in your wallet or handbag, as the case may be.[66]

The deceased . . .	DEATH IS GOOD	DEATH IS BAD
. . . owed you money		x
. . . was owed money by you	x	
. . . signed for packages in your absence		x
. . . called the cops when your dog barked	x	
. . . had the job you want	x	
. . . wanted your job	x	

See? It's easy! With that in mind, let's dip into the archives and reexamine three different death-related scenarios.

When Loved Ones Pass Away

Consider the dilemma faced when a friend or acquaintance dies. This was the situation confronted by Mrs. A. D. of Elmira, N.Y., when she wrote to me back in July 1996:

....

66. Do not actually do this. Doing this involves theft of valuable intellectual property and will result in immediate, costly, back-breaking litigation.

> My elderly neighbor Mr. Witmer
> recently passed away after a
> long illness. I didn't know him
> well, although we exchanged
> greetings for years, took in each
> other's mail, and so forth. Still,
> I've been surprised at my grief.
> It's almost like a member of my
> own family passed. Can you
> help?

Mrs. A. D. blunders onto a key phrase here: "My grief." *My* grief. When a friend dies one must remember that though others are suffering, maybe even others who were closer to the decedent—wives, husbands, children—there is no one whose grief is more potent or meaningful than yours. Thus it is only right to expect everyone with whom you come into contact at this time to bend Heaven and Earth to make you feel better. But people can be selfish, especially when they think they're grieving. For that reason, you need to ensure that everyone understands how much more important your grief is than theirs. This takes a plan. Fortunately, I have one. Let's send Mrs. A. D. on a condolence call to the Witmer family wake.

She enters the living room. What's the first thing she sees? Witmer family members crying inconsolably, hugging one another, trading warm family memories, and generally stealing focus from her own extrafamilial grief. She must act quickly. Barely inside the door, she drops to her knees and begins wailing: "Why, why, why? Why did he have to do this to me? I'm his neighbor and he left me all alone!" This has the added benefit of introducing Mrs. A. D. to family members she has never met, which in this case sounds like all of them, while establishing the primacy of her grief. Why, she lived right next door, and some of these mourner-come-latelies—the dead man's children, for example—didn't even care enough to live in the same city!

"Good manners" will engage now, and a family member will almost certainly come to Mrs. A. D. and offer her a hand up. Let's say it's the late Mr. Witmer's sister. Mrs. A. D. should shove the woman's helping hand away and struggle to her feet unaided, as if to personify the plucky persistence that will help her move beyond her debilitating grief. The sister will most likely introduce herself at this point. Mrs. A. D. should now be gracious. "He loved you so much, you know," she should gasp through her tears.

"Thank you," the sister may say. "How did you know Herb?"

"Who?"

"My brother. *Herb*," she'll say, gesturing vaguely in the direction of the casket.

"Oh, *Herb*," Mrs. A. D. will sob, cueing another round of lamentations. The sister will in all likelihood edge away from her now, making this a good time to make a move toward the casket. She should feel free to chant the dead man's name like a mantra as she moves across the floor, especially now that she knows it, which is a nice plus. Upon arriving at the casket, she should move behind it, then fall across it, her head toward the assembled mourners, as she offers yet more wordless keening. This is really her chance to shine, because if she's doing her job correctly no one will be able to ignore her now. If she's so inclined, and I encourage it, it would not be out of line at this point to consider speaking in tongues.[67] A nearly transcendent, quasi-rapturous expression of grief—that's what we're after here.

Time to take a break. Mrs. A. D. should gather herself, dry her tears, straighten her seams. This would be a good time to choke down some coffee and cake, and believe me, she will have no competition at the food table. Indeed, if she's done her job correctly, she will be surrounded for the remainder of her visit by a sort of jellyfish-like force field which will enforce a people-free perimeter around her as she moves through the room. She should

....

67. Suggestions: "Aka-lacka Meschach," "Oh Lord a-walla-walla-walla," "Humminy bumminy ooOOOOOOOooooo, ooOOOOOOOooooo." Repeat as necessary.

make this work to her advantage, wandering distractedly from corner to corner, muttering the dead man's name. (A reminder: it's Herb.) She should now have a majority of mourners convinced that Mr. Witmer's passing was such a blow that it has unmoored her from reality, and she will spend the balance of her days an actual grief-crippled madwoman.

It's curtain time. She should now begin moving toward the exit, sending up one last great exhalation of mourning as she reaches the door. (This would also be a good time to check for her keys.) Once there she should fall silent, square her shoulders as if to imply a brave acceptance of the new, post-Witmer world in which she's forced to live, and exit quietly, secure in the knowledge that for the eight to 10 minutes of her appearance, no one in the room has been more grief-stricken than she. That's a small thing, but it's going to have to be her comfort now.

When Enemies Die

In late August 1999 I received this letter from Mrs. A. L. of West Covina, Calif.:

> After the recent death of my
> boss, everyone in the office was
> invited to a memorial service. It
> seemed clear from the invitation

> that attendance was expected. I
> don't want to speak ill of the
> dead, but my late boss and I had
> many conflicts over the years
> and it seems hypocritical to
> think of going. Am I obligated to
> attend?

I remember it as if it were yesterday. I remember
that I spent much of late August 1999 pretending to be a
nightclub psychic, clutching my brow in mock concentration, frowning, and muttering, "I'm getting a picture. I'm
seeing . . . *the doormat of the office*, am I right? Let me
guess: you're the mousy middle manager who always gets
conned into punching in for the young secretary who
can't get in on time and always looks tired in the mornings, as if she's been having waaaaaaay more fun than your
parched powers of imagination allow you to picture. Am I
right? *Thank* you!" Honestly, I had Debbie in stitches. I
even went so far as to send her out in search of a reason-
ably priced used turban, thinking it might make for an
amusing afternoon in the office in lieu of actual work. But
all it got me was a grumpier-than-usual assistant and an
angry lecture on the creeps and lowlifes who hang out in
thrift shops.

Let me now expand on the answer I gave Mrs. A. L.
in my column: Madam, the mere fact that you need to

write to me for an answer is itself an answer. It says—or it would say, if you were as attuned to your Inner Crank® as you doubtless are to *Fear Factor* and the crapulent wallpaperings of Thomas Kinkade, the Painter of Light—that you already know what to do and are desperately trying to convince yourself it's okay. Do you know how many hours you spend every week in this wasted effort? I do: studies have shown that it's upwards of 12. Most of them are spent on Monday mornings, Friday afternoons, and all day Wednesdays, when an office drone like yourself is statistically most likely to be hating the very life she lives. Now ask yourself this: how many hours a week does Mr. Irresponsible spend trying to convince himself to do something he doesn't feel like doing? If you answered "none," "zero," "not any," or "nil," you are absolutely correct. In any given week, I spend more time trying to pry the raisins from my cinnamon buns than I do grappling with the intricacies of moral obligation.

With that in mind, let's reconsider Mrs. A. L.'s dilemma. The boss has died; a boss-related social obligation looms, and with it a question: Should Mrs. A. L. spend the afternoon in the stuffy confines of a rented Unitarian church, the faint aroma of congealing potato salad wafting up from the rec room below, feigning grief over the permanent removal from her life of a man she despised? Or should she aim her Dodge Dart south from West Covina and head straight for Disneyland, where she can spend the afternoon on the Pirates of the Caribbean ride, lustily belting out "A pirate's life for me" and eating chocolate-covered frozen bananas? We have here what trained observers of human behavior call "a no-brainer." All you need do is look at the querulous tone of the question itself: she and the late boss were "not close," yet she still uncoils herself from the armadillo-like self-defensive posture he inspires, even in death, to question her duty. Are we seeing love here, or devotion, or even the professional respect one colleague affords another? No, what we are seeing is fear, the kind of primitive survival instinct a cat feels tickling at its neural pathways when it sees a dog, or a homeowner feels when the doorbell rings and it's Jehovah's Witnesses.

Consider what this says about the character of her late boss. (Let's call him "Mr. Torquemada," because it's funny.) We can safely surmise that he was a cruel, manipulative man, a dime store Mussolini in cheap suits and crêpe-soled shoes, the kind of petty tyrant who returns from "working dinners" at the Olive Garden reeking of cheap Chianti and clams oreganato, delighted at the way his browbeaten minions dive for cover, burying their heads in spreadsheets and invoices, avoiding his eye, lying low. Now he's reaching out from beyond the grave to exercise a last measure of bullying, brutalizing mind control. If Mrs. A. L. were standing before me I would scream, because I live in a gated community and the guards are supposed to pick off intruders before they ever get near my house, and Debbie has specific instructions to set the dogs on anybody who approaches the porch. But after I stopped screaming I would tell her this: Lady, there is no way your life isn't demonstrably better with Mr. Torquemada filing his next 10 million annual employee evaluations from a corner office with a view of the River Styx. Go kick up your heels and celebrate.

The lessons of this approach are obvious, and the benefits clear. When God or the fates or the universe see fit to expunge from your field of view a person who has caused you only misery, don't look at the spot where they used to stand and ask why. Look at the clear vista of self-enriching possibility stretching out ahead, and gun your engines.

Is Now the Right Moment to Pick a Fight with Family Members?

Mr. Irresponsible wouldn't be able to sleep at night if he failed to bring up something delicate, and believe me, you do *not* want Mr. Irresponsible walking around all groggy and snappish. The bad news is this: family members die, and when they do all manner of family resentments bubble to the surface like marsh gas. Take this letter from the unfortunate Ms. D. B. C. of Marietta, Ga.:

> My mother recently passed
> away, and of course we were all
> upset. But I don't think that's
> any excuse for what happened
> after the funeral. We all went
> back to my house for coffee and
> cake and my brother Al got into
> the Scotch and before anybody
> really knew what was happening
> he and our sister Janis were
> standing in the middle of the liv-
> ing room screaming at each
> other about who mom loved
> more. Lord, it was awful. My
> husband Jeff managed to sepa-
> rate them but I still felt embar-
> rassed. Now Janis and Al aren't
> speaking to each other and I feel
> like I ought to do something to
> try to get them back together.
> Should I?

This letter crossed my desk in the winter of 2000, which has given me some time to reconsider the advice I gave Ms. D. B. C. I haven't, of course, because one of my rules is never to reconsider a piece of advice. That doesn't mean I can't expand on it, however.

Family relationships may be likened to a house of cards (except in the respect that an actual house of cards is infinitely more stable and robust). Remove one relational card and you can bet the whole thing will come crashing down. Soak that metaphoric card in Scotch and nostalgia and unresolved feelings of envy and guilt and shame and it will burst into flames as you tug at it, scorching your fingertips and threatening to burn down your entire emotional apartment building.

In other words, family funerals and the social gatherings that follow them are virtual tinderboxes. They are 100 percent guaranteed, a mortal lock, to end in screams and recrimination. Thus the advice I gave to Ms. D. B. C.—as I recall, it was along the lines of "Get over it and leave me alone"—simply didn't go far enough. What I should have said is: Look at this as an opportunity. Given the way the thing is going to go, why not get out in front of it? You're going to end the day pulling somebody off somebody, tallying up the count of things said that can never be taken back, and trying your best to get whiskey stains out of a dark blue suit.[68] Doesn't it make sense to turn the tide to your own advantage? That way, at least

....

68. Mr. Irresponsible recommends that you mix equal parts white vinegar and water, apply to the stain, and blot.

one person is going to get something off her chest and feel a little better.

Here's how it can work: Let's say you've just put Aunt Winnie in the ground and the family has convened at your cousin Barbara's house. Have *one* drink, not more—just enough to give you that warm, confident, "Bring it on" feeling, but not so much that your tongue thickens or your wits flag. Take a position from which you can observe everyone in the room. Now stand back and wait. Smoke 'em if you got 'em. Bide your time. Your chance is coming. Hang on, what's this? . . . Barbara's sister Judy is staring down at the crab puff in her hand. She seems to be trying to will it to talk. She isn't moving, unless you count the slight counterclockwise rotation of her torso over her planted feet. Wait for it. . . . Now her watery eyes widen and she looks around the room, fixing at last on Barbara. Her eyebrows gather themselves into a "V." She drops the crab puff to the carpet[69] and starts steaming purposefully toward her unsuspecting sister. It's showtime.

The trick here is to let Judy open her mouth—so that later, during the many inevitable post-party recount-

....

69. Soak the spot with a peroxide-and-detergent solution for five minutes. Then, using a clean white absorbent cloth, blot the area, pressing down firmly for 30 seconds. Do not rub.

ings of the ugly incident, it isn't you who gets the blame for striking the match—but *not to let her get very far.* So let Judy struggle all the way across the floor to Barbara and launch into the beginnings of what's sure to be a crazy, incoherent rant about Mom and Dad and that time at the lake and how Barbara always— And right here, as soon as you hear the word "always," signaling that Judy is about to dip a toe into the rip tides of habitual family behavior, tides from which no one has ever been pulled, this is your signal to strike. The sound of the magic word "always" will have Barbara stiffened to counterattack. Now unleash your Inner Crank® and let her fly!

It doesn't matter so much what you say. The guests will have been on high alert for trouble, like twitchy National Guardsmen at airport security checkpoints. Their attention will have shifted rapidly to Judy as the incident began, and it will remain fixed there for at least a few moments more. So go nuts! Dust off ancient slights from grade school days, slander relatives who aren't there, stir up trouble, leverage sibling rivalries for your own advantage. But do it quickly, in a torrid burst, and then grab your car keys and dash for the door. By the time everyone realizes what's happened you'll be on your way to Wendy's for a quick bite, leaving Judy to reap a whirl-wind of blame for what will already be going down in family lore as "When Judy started that huge fight after Aunt Winnie's funeral." You'll feel as if you've dropped 30 pounds of ugly flab, for in a sense that's exactly what you've done—you've shed a great weight of emotional baggage and let somebody else take the blame. It's what Aunt Winnie would have wanted.

Chapter

The 10 Commandments of Bad Advice

It should be apparent, if you've read this far, that Mr. Irresponsible believes in the easy answer. The easy answer has gotten a bad rap in our culture of advice-giving, which holds that problems are myriad, that they eat themselves and multiply, and that modern life tends toward ever more complicated social interactions demanding ever more complex solutions. This is hooey. I believe that every one of us knows exactly what to do at every second—that the voice of the Inner Crank® lives in each of us despite our efforts to reason it away. It's been my hope that this book will help you tune into that voice, tune out the gabble and blather of the Advice Culture, and listen to your own most basic human instincts: self-preservation, self-gratification, and an overarching tendency toward what might be called "enlightened bitterness." I've done my best to make the preceding chapters as succinctly selfish as possible. But, if the arguments I've made are somehow still too nuanced for you—who loves you, baby? Mr. Irresponsible, that's who, despite all appearances to the contrary. Herewith, a book's worth of advice boiled down to bite-sized, easily digestible snippets.

1. Bad manners have a cure, and the cure is worse manners. When someone violates commonly held dicta of acceptable behavior, they must for the greater good be corrected. But such persons are by definition self-involved and thick-headed, and so you will need to get their attention. Act badly. Permission granted. At the end of the day you will have increased, not lessened, the quotient of good manners in the world. (Besides, it's fun.)

2. Use force if you have to. Whether it's the attention-getting finger-flick or the steel rod across the bridge of the nose, there isn't anybody who doesn't respond to a little something that says, "Eyes front, mister." Remember: It's *loving* to offer a little well-meaning advice. You don't want to waste your love, do you?

3. Family is a barnacle. Family does nothing to speed your way through the waters of life. It only slows you down, and when you try to pry it off the hull of your existence it cuts the fingers of your best intentions with the razor-sharp shell of guilt and shame. You know what you need? One of those shiny aluminum-hulled fishing boats. Yeah. That'd be sweet. Let's see your family try to plant themselves on *that*.

4. Win. You think you're right, don't you? Sure you do. Everybody does. So doesn't it stand to reason that everybody should think like you do? Sure it does. Don't you want everybody to be right? Not for your sake alone, but for theirs too? Mostly for yours, but a little bit for theirs? Sure you do.

5. Money cures all. Don't listen to utopian hogwash like "All you need is love." I've checked; love is notoriously poor at keeping your house cool in summer and warm in winter. The lady behind the counter at the electric company may be flattered, even charmed, if you offer her a sincere hug come next winter, but you will nevertheless end up staring at an inoperative TV in a cold, dark house.

6. Death is not the worst thing that can happen to you. Other people are. Sartre wrote that "Hell is other people." He may not have been the guy you want to go to Vegas with for Memorial Day weekend, but he was right on the money here. Other people are the things that prevent a pure adherence to the cleansing principles of self-interest. They are the ruts in your path, the speed bumps on your highway, the stones in your kidney. They must be cleared from your way, flattened, or pulverized with ultrasound.

7. Love isn't blue. It's black. There are worse things than being alone, and one of them is what social scientists call "the mushy surrender." Love clouds your judgment and directs your psychic gaze toward others, where it has no business going. Worse, it prompts terrible, unnatural thoughts of self-sacrifice—of "caring for someone else more than you care for yourself." This may be fine in Happyland, where the sky is always a cloudless azure and cartoon bluebirds sing tweet-tweet-tweet all the livelong day, but you know what? You don't live in Happyland. You live in Detroit, and you need to watch your step. Let the "love of your life" watch hers.

8. Don't listen to anybody. Maybe there aren't really 10 Commandments of Bad Advice. Maybe there are only, say, eight.

Afterword

That's the ballgame. Mr. Irresponsible hopes you put down this slim but useful volume and return to the world a better, more fully evolved and creatively self-centered person. The great Dutch analyst Dr. Piers Groopman once wrote, *"Zich bekijken is alles; anderen bekijken is een shonda"* ("To look at oneself is everything; to look at others is a shonda"). If I've done my job right, this book will have triggered a round of narcissistic navel-gazing unprecedented since your teenage years.

This is right. It is just. For it is only by looking at ourselves that we can hope to truly shut out others, with their problems and failures, none of which is personally our fault. If Mr. Irresponsible had his way, the human race would be freed forever from the false notion that we are our brothers' keepers. Think of it! A trillion tiny nation-states! A people that spend their days gazing relentlessly inward and downward, focused firmly on the orderly procession of their own steps toward tomorrow! Aside from the bumping into each other, it's a beautiful picture. That is the future I wish for you. But much, much more importantly, it is the future I wish for me.

Mr. Irresponsible will
return in early 2006 in
**Mr. Irresponsible 2 . . .
I Loved
You Tuesday**